CHER AMI:

WWI Homing Pigeon

Written by Joeming Dunn • Illustrated by Ben Dunn

FAMOUS FIRSTS: ANIMALS MAKING HISTORY

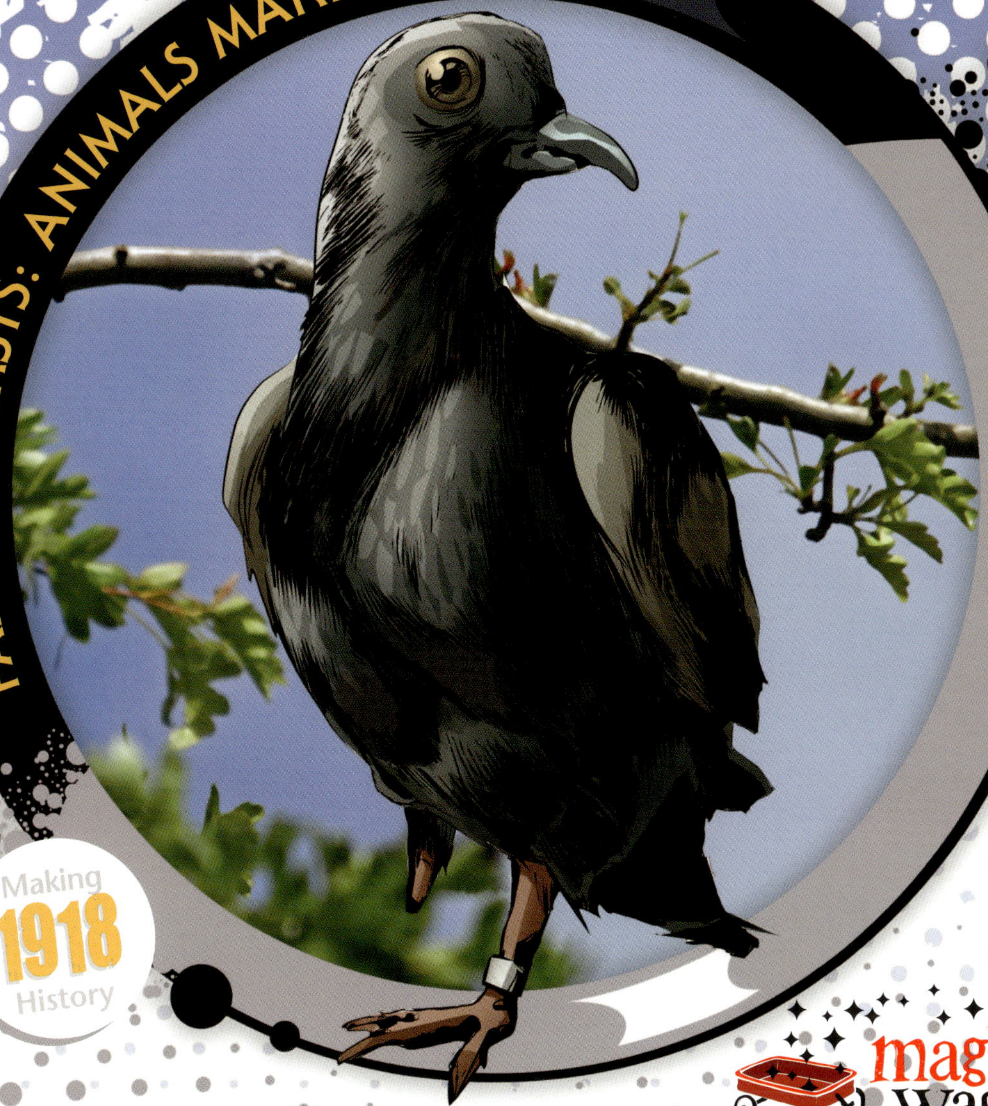

Making 1918 History

magic wagon

visit us at www.abdopublishing.com

Published by Magic Wagon, a division of the ABDO Publishing Group, 8000 West 78th Street, Edina, Minnesota 55439. Copyright © 2012 by Abdo Consulting Group, Inc. International copyrights reserved in all countries. All rights reserved. No part of this book may be reproduced in any form without written permission from the publisher.

Graphic Planet™ is a trademark and logo of Magic Wagon.

Printed in the United States of America, North Mankato, Minnesota.
052011
092011
 This book contains at least 10% recycled materials.

Written by Joeming Dunn
Illustrated by Ben Dunn
Colored by Robby Bevard
Lettered by Doug Dlin
Edited by Stephanie Hedlund and Rochelle Baltzer
Interior layout and design by Antarctic Press
Cover art by Brian Denham
Cover design by Neil Klinepier

Library of Congress Cataloging-in-Publication Data

Dunn, Joeming W.
  Cher Ami : WWI homing pigeon / written by Joeming Dunn ; illustrated by Ben Dunn.
    p. cm. -- (Famous firsts: animals making history)
  Includes index.
  ISBN 978-1-61641-639-3
  1. Cher Ami (Pigeon)--Juvenile literature. 2. Homing pigeons--War use--United States--History--20th century--Juvenile literature. 3. World War, 1914-1918--Communications--Juvenile literature. 4. Famous animals--Juvenile literature. I. Dunn, Ben, ill. II. Title.
  D639.P45D86 2012
  940.4'12730929--dc22
                                        2011011064

TABLE OF CONTENTS

War Begins..............................5
War Messengers 8
Advance on the Charlevaux Valley 12
Cher Ami to the Rescue 18
The Homing Pigeon Returns...............26
Cher Ami Facts 30
Web Sites 30
Glossary 31
Index 32

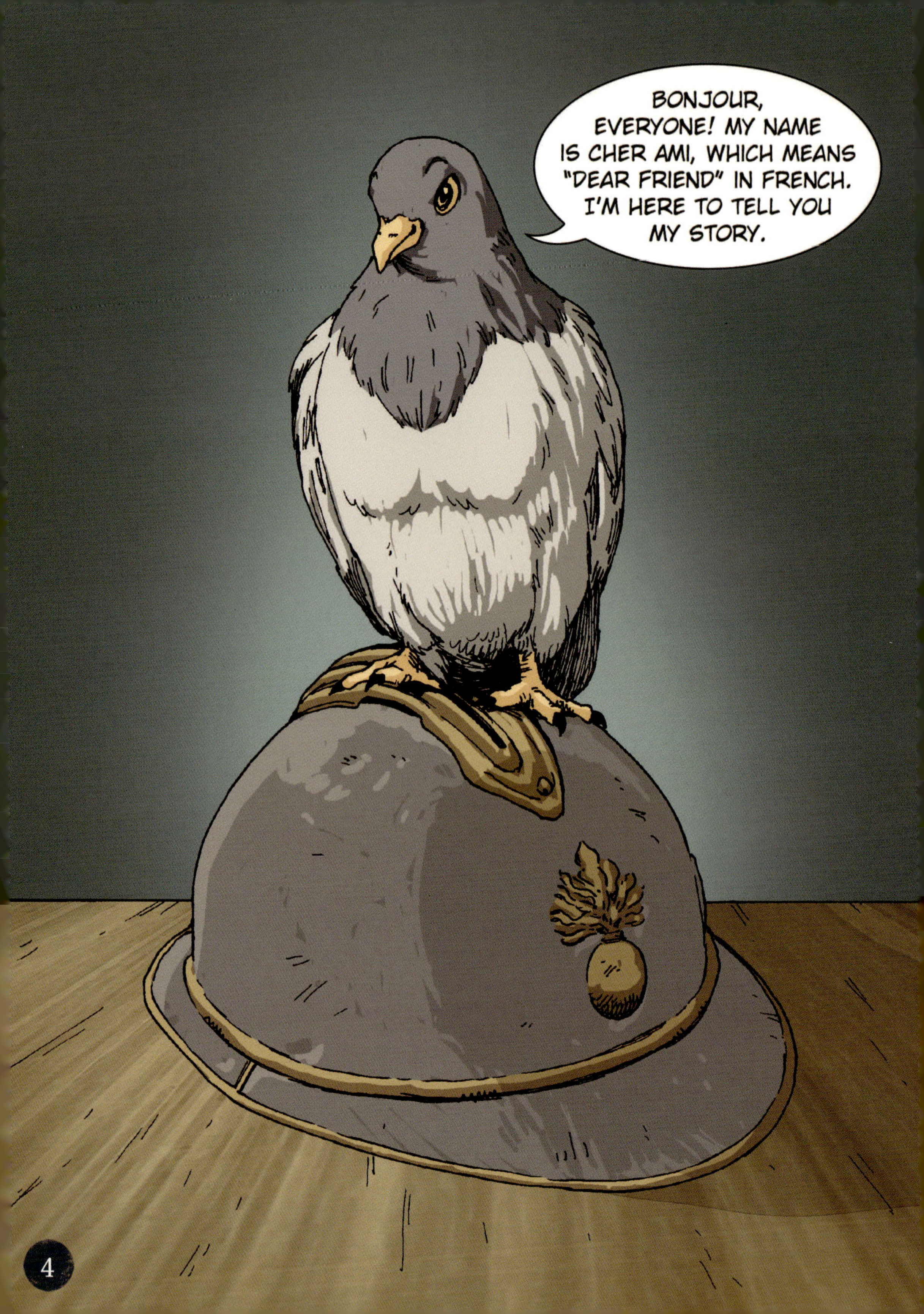
BONJOUR, EVERYONE! MY NAME IS CHER AMI, WHICH MEANS "DEAR FRIEND" IN FRENCH. I'M HERE TO TELL YOU MY STORY.

WAR BEGINS

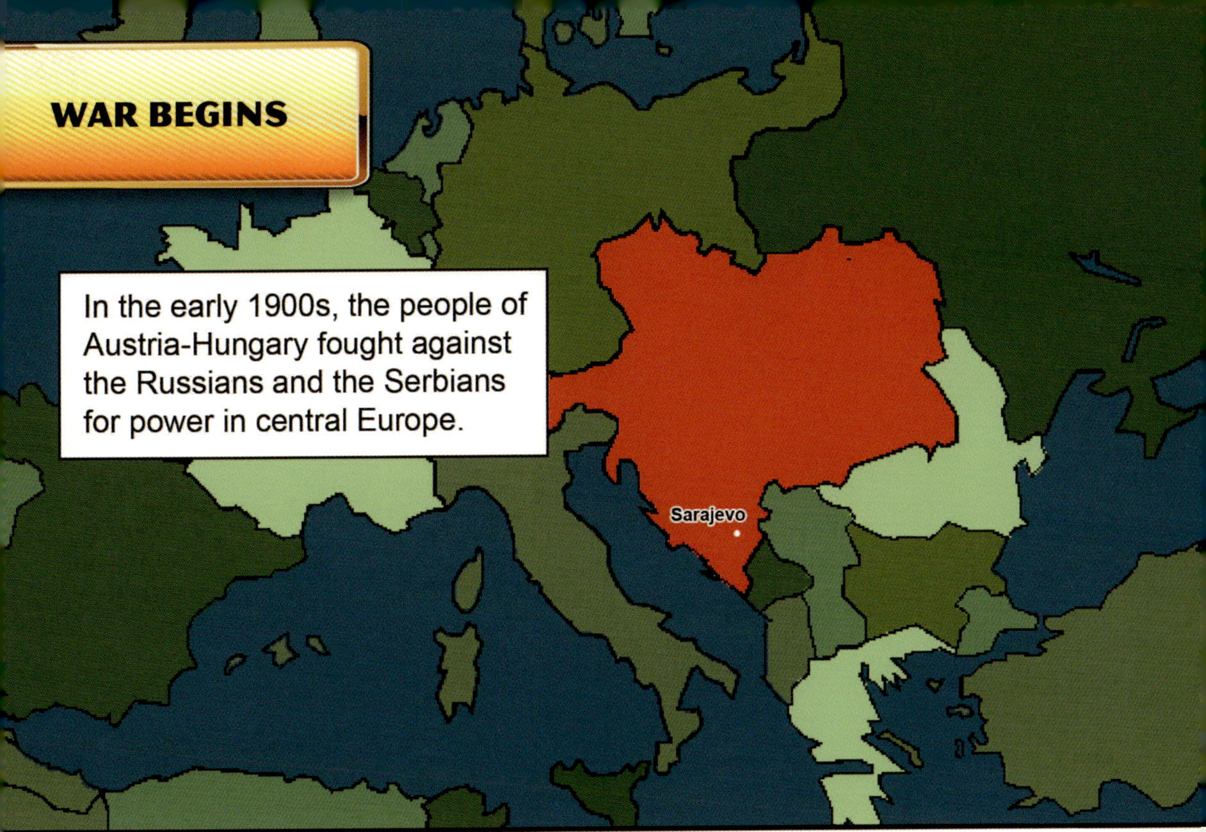
In the early 1900s, the people of Austria-Hungary fought against the Russians and the Serbians for power in central Europe.
Sarajevo

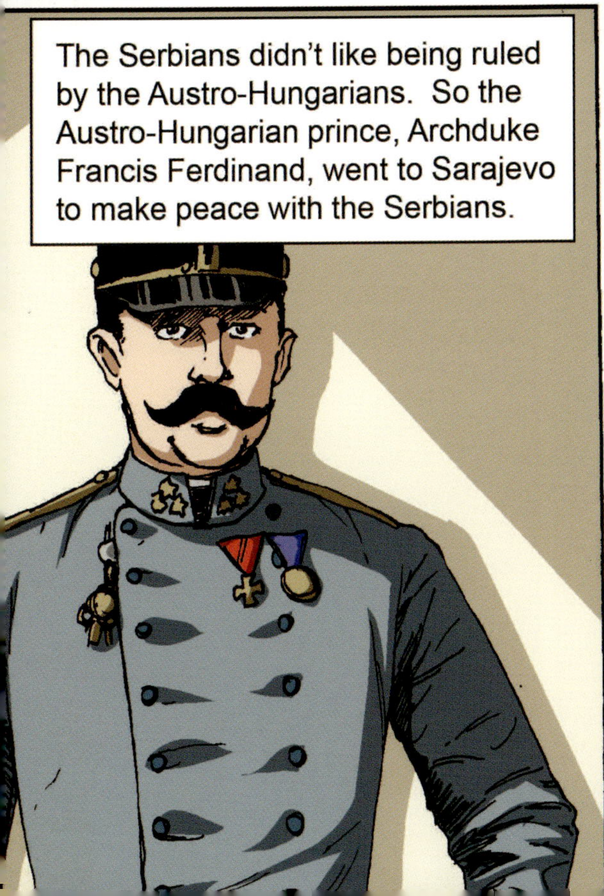
The Serbians didn't like being ruled by the Austro-Hungarians. So the Austro-Hungarian prince, Archduke Francis Ferdinand, went to Sarajevo to make peace with the Serbians.

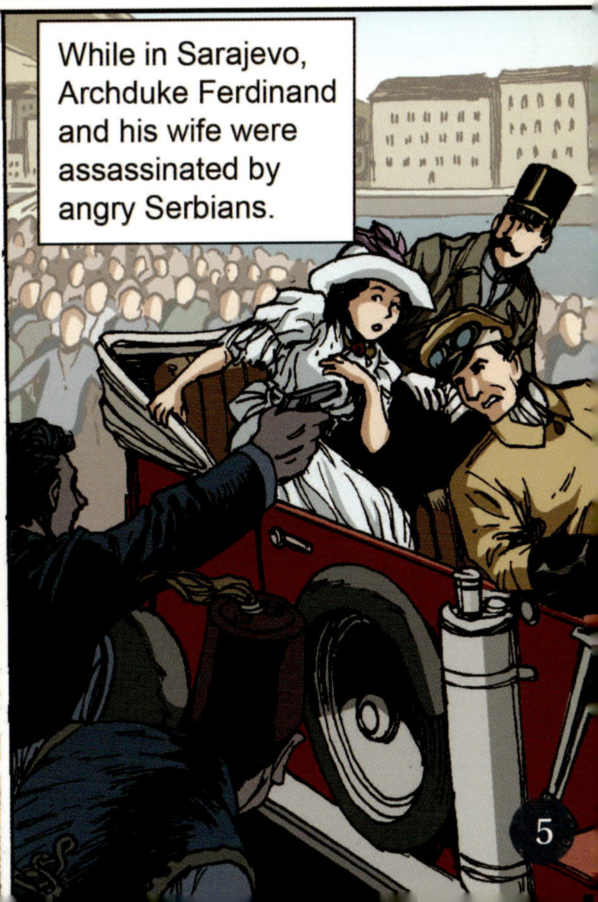
While in Sarajevo, Archduke Ferdinand and his wife were assassinated by angry Serbians.

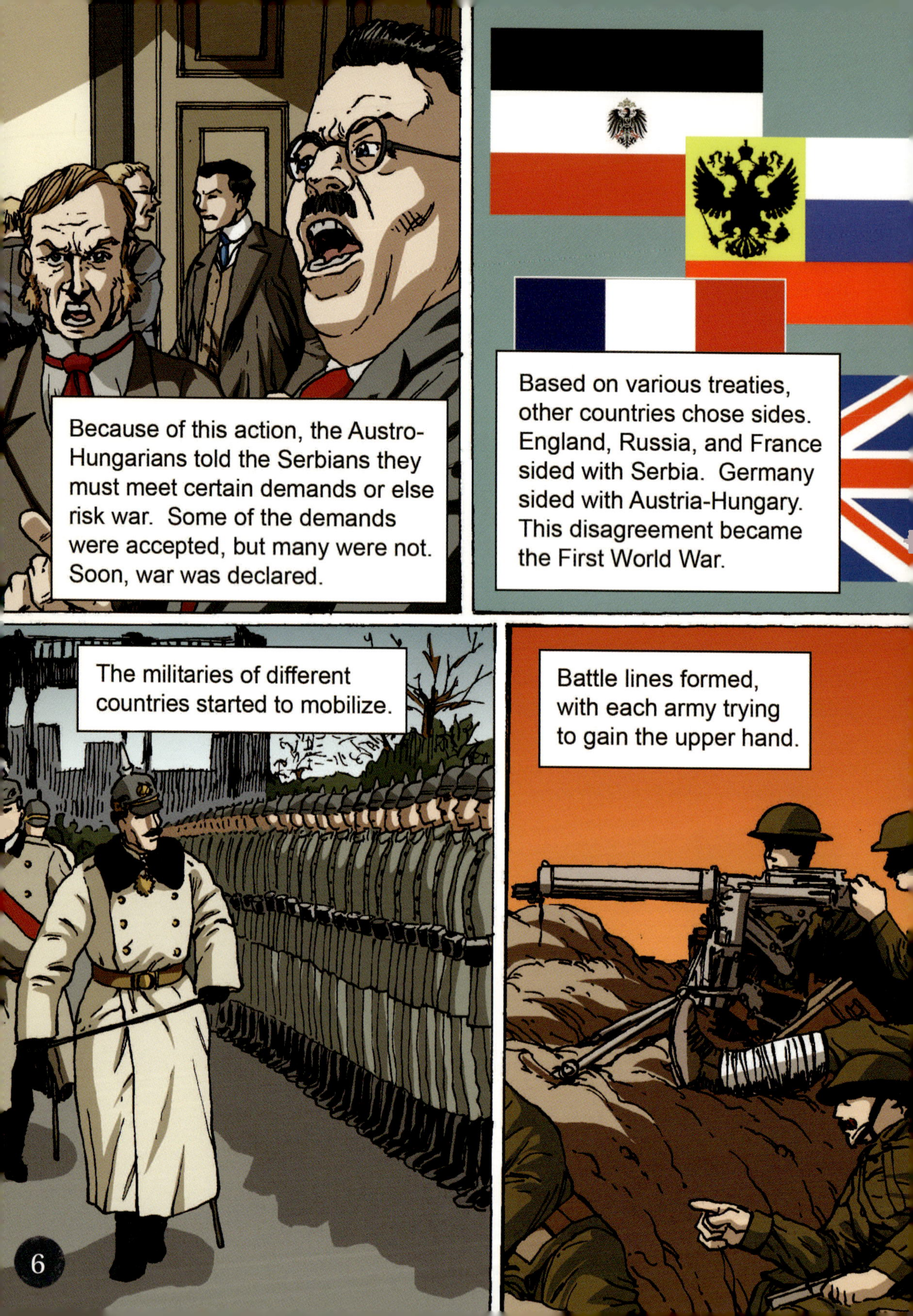
Because of this action, the Austro-Hungarians told the Serbians they must meet certain demands or else risk war. Some of the demands were accepted, but many were not. Soon, war was declared.
Based on various treaties, other countries chose sides. England, Russia, and France sided with Serbia. Germany sided with Austria-Hungary. This disagreement became the First World War.
The militaries of different countries started to mobilize.
Battle lines formed, with each army trying to gain the upper hand.

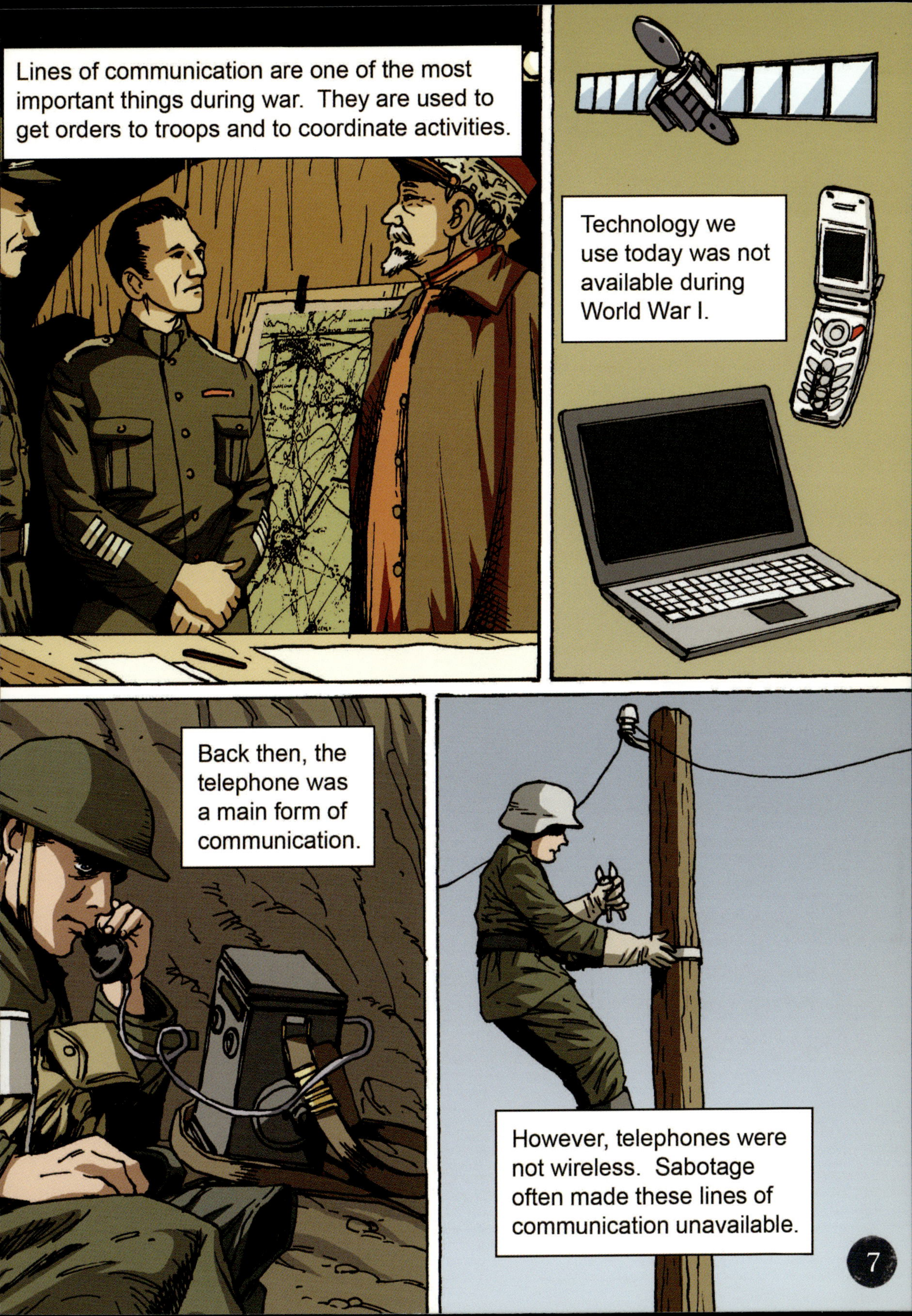
Lines of communication are one of the most important things during war. They are used to get orders to troops and to coordinate activities.
Technology we use today was not available during World War I.
Back then, the telephone was a main form of communication.
However, telephones were not wireless. Sabotage often made these lines of communication unavailable.

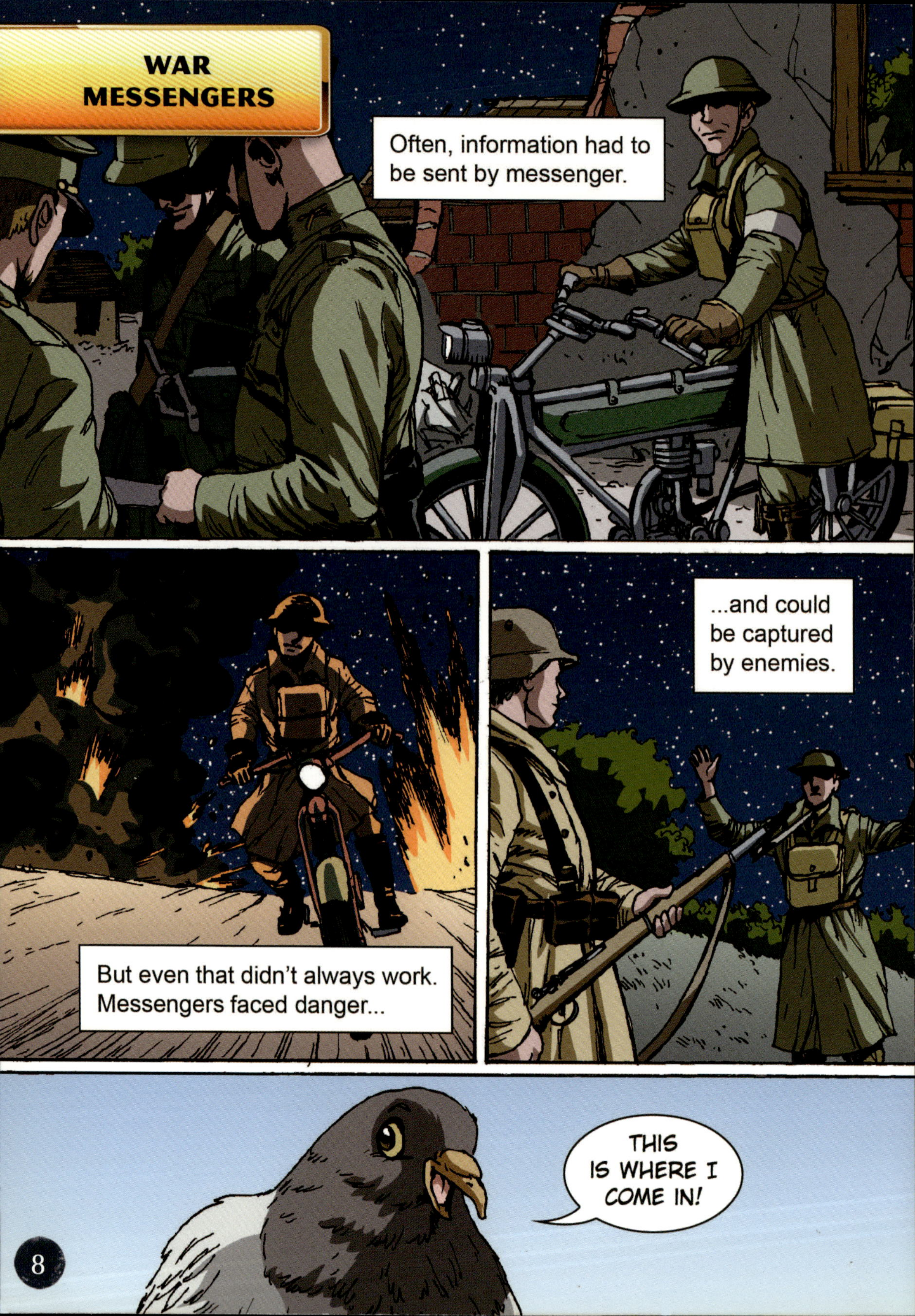
WAR MESSENGERS
Often, information had to be sent by messenger.
But even that didn't always work. Messengers faced danger...
...and could be captured by enemies.
THIS IS WHERE I COME IN!

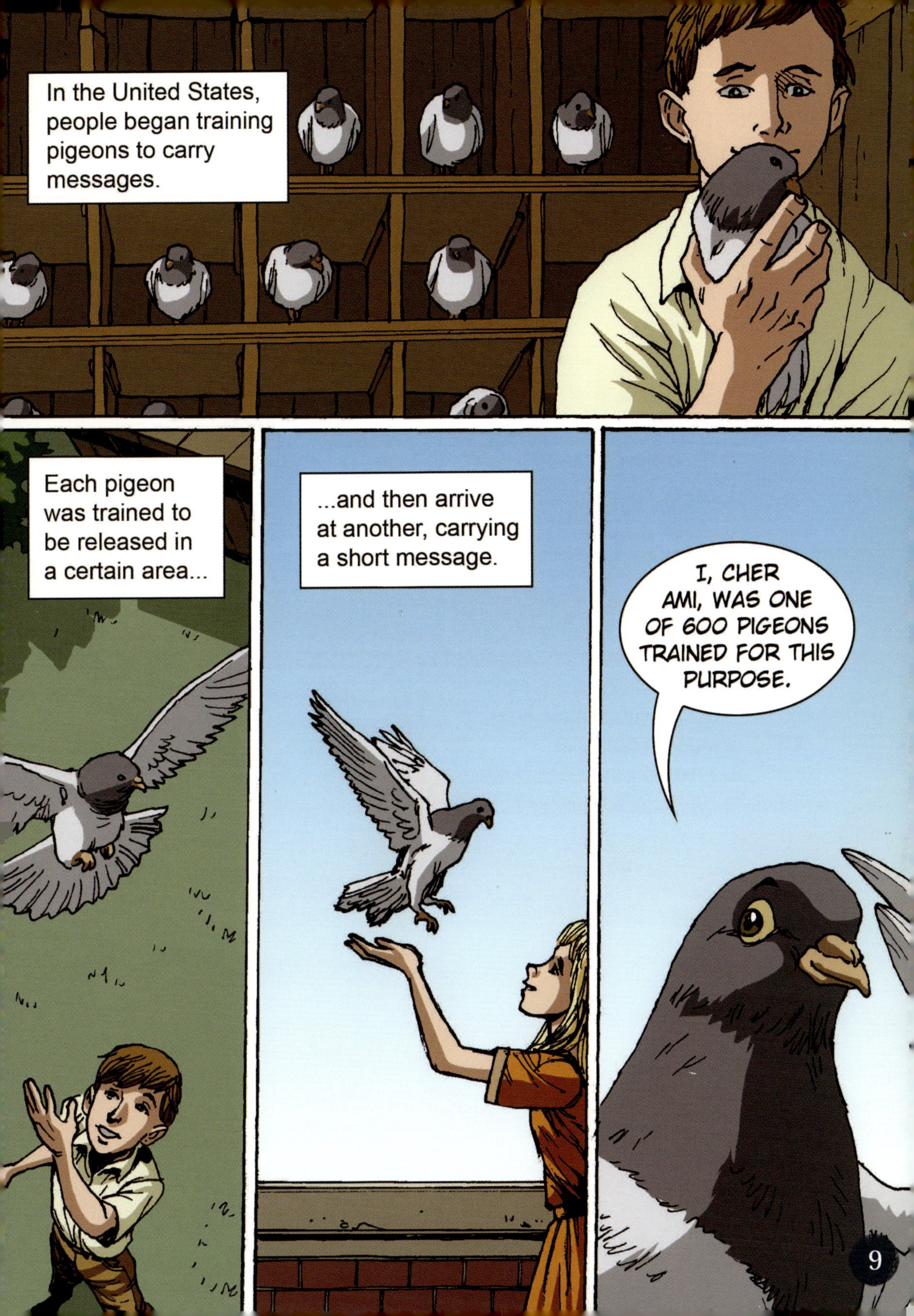

In the United States, people began training pigeons to carry messages.
Each pigeon was trained to be released in a certain area...
...and then arrive at another, carrying a short message.
I, CHER AMI, WAS ONE OF 600 PIGEONS TRAINED FOR THIS PURPOSE.

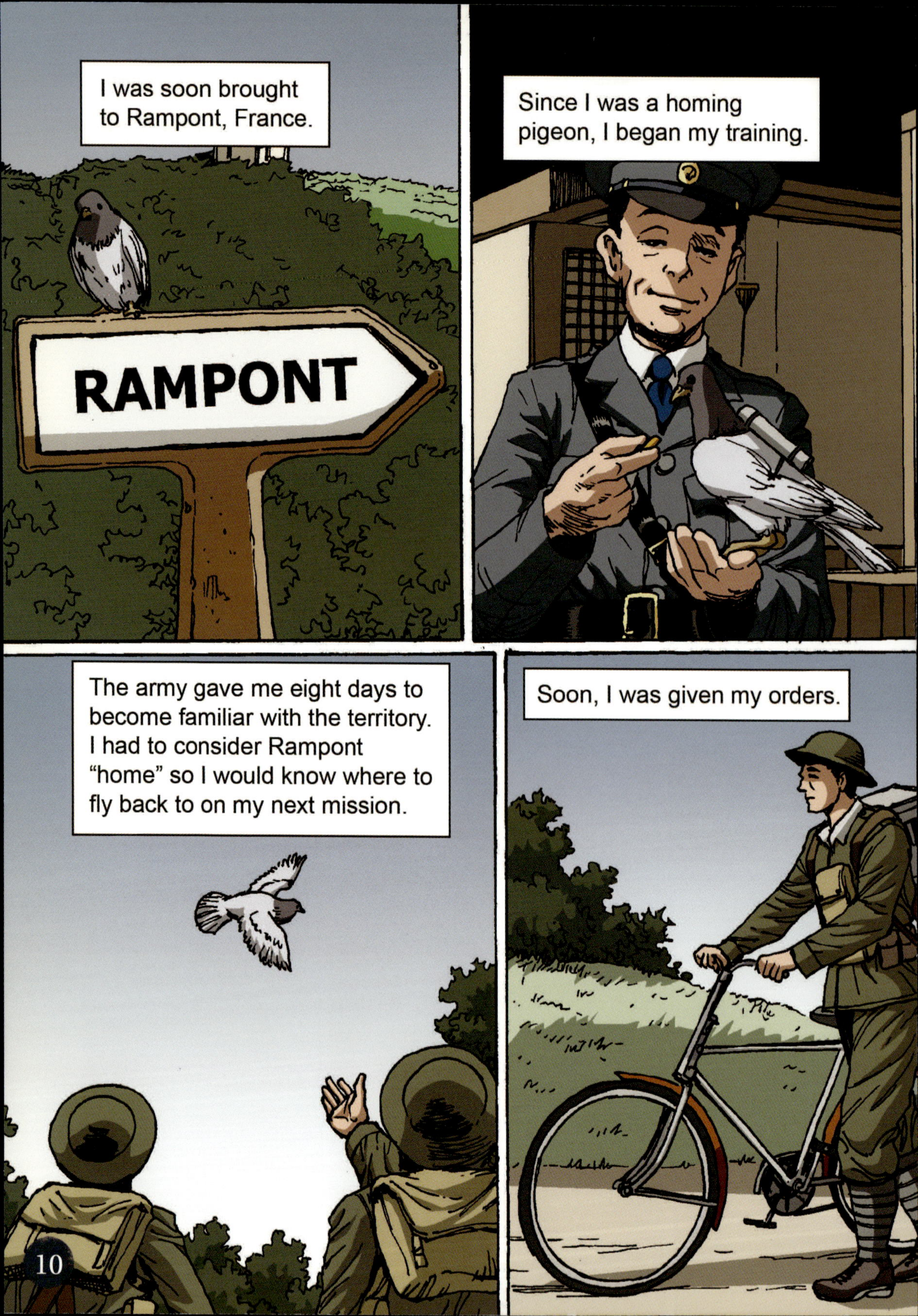
I was soon brought to Rampont, France.
RAMPONT
Since I was a homing pigeon, I began my training.
The army gave me eight days to become familiar with the territory. I had to consider Rampont "home" so I would know where to fly back to on my next mission.
Soon, I was given my orders.

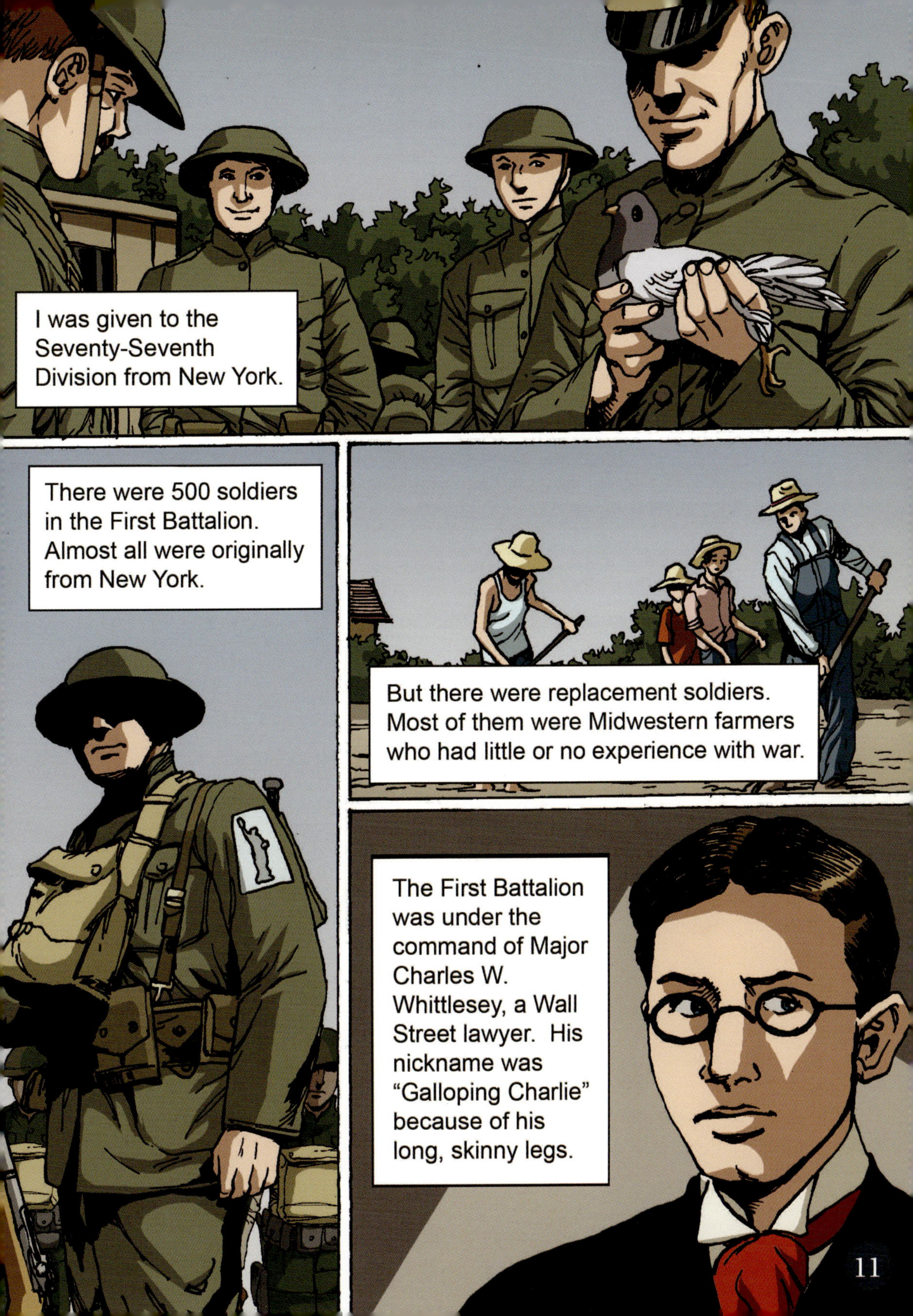
I was given to the Seventy-Seventh Division from New York.
There were 500 soldiers in the First Battalion. Almost all were originally from New York.
But there were replacement soldiers. Most of them were Midwestern farmers who had little or no experience with war.
The First Battalion was under the command of Major Charles W. Whittlesey, a Wall Street lawyer. His nickname was "Galloping Charlie" because of his long, skinny legs.

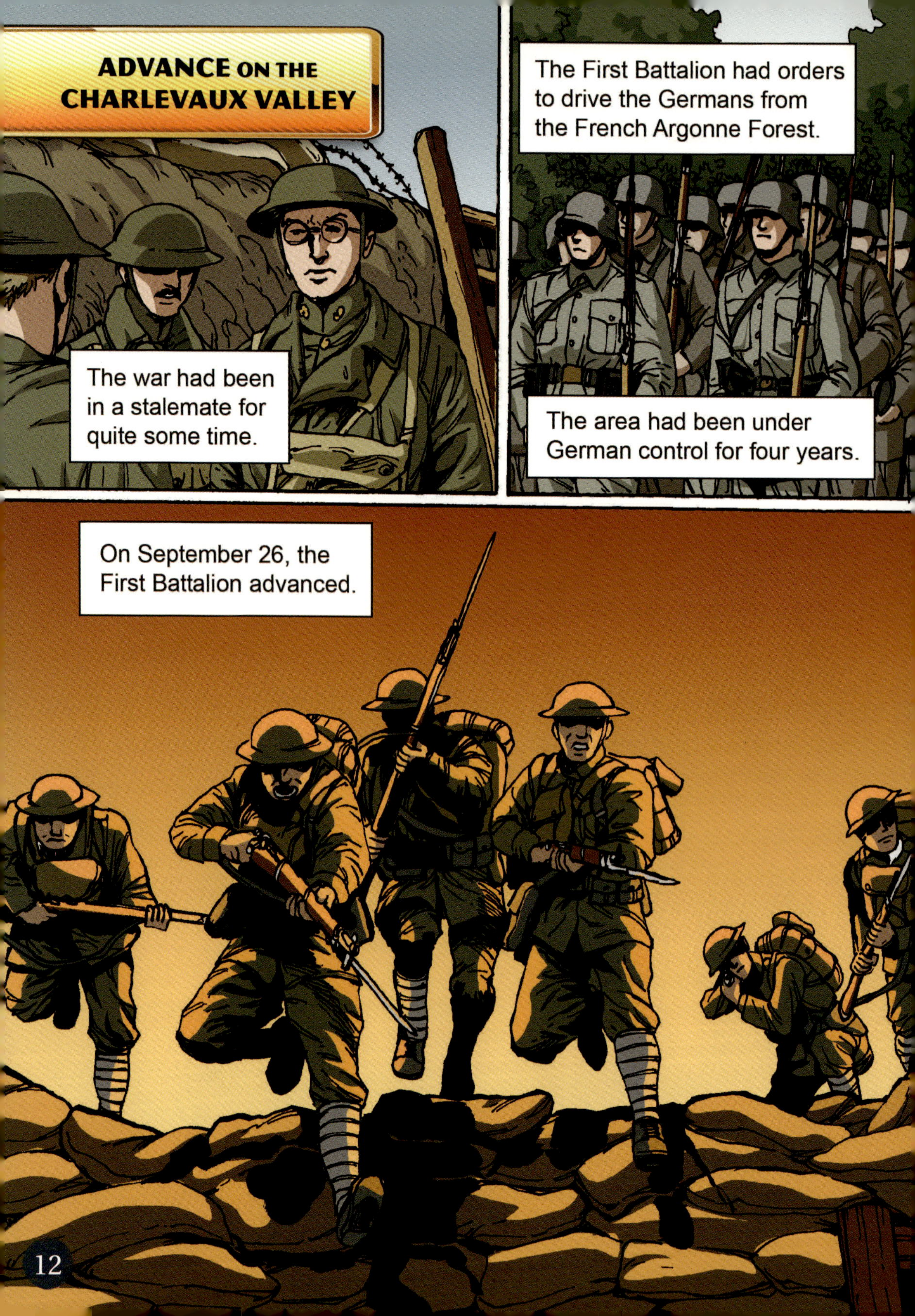
ADVANCE ON THE CHARLEVAUX VALLEY
The war had been in a stalemate for quite some time.
The First Battalion had orders to drive the Germans from the French Argonne Forest.
The area had been under German control for four years.
On September 26, the First Battalion advanced.

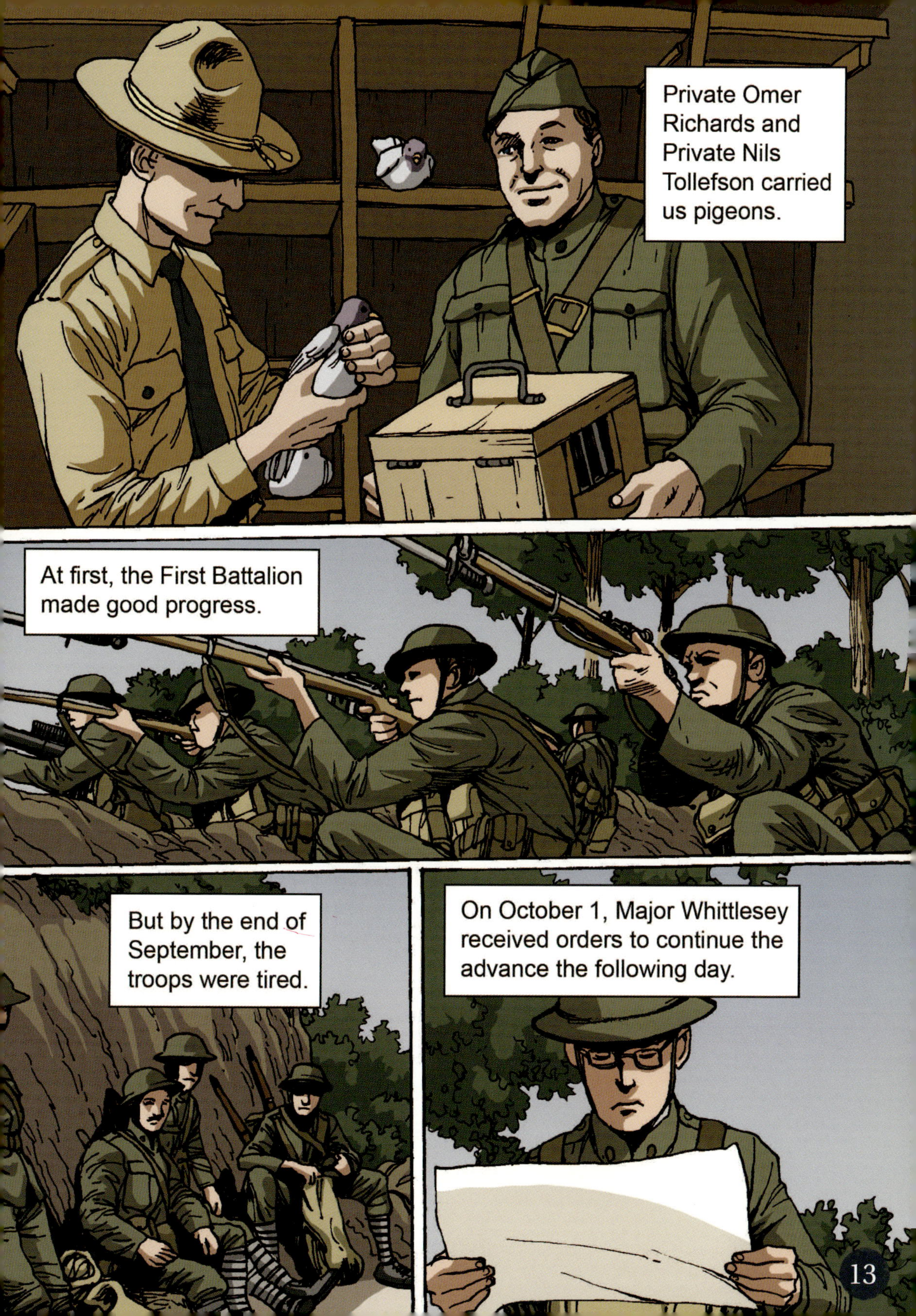
Private Omer Richards and Private Nils Tollefson carried us pigeons.
At first, the First Battalion made good progress.
But by the end of September, the troops were tired.
On October 1, Major Whittlesey received orders to continue the advance the following day.

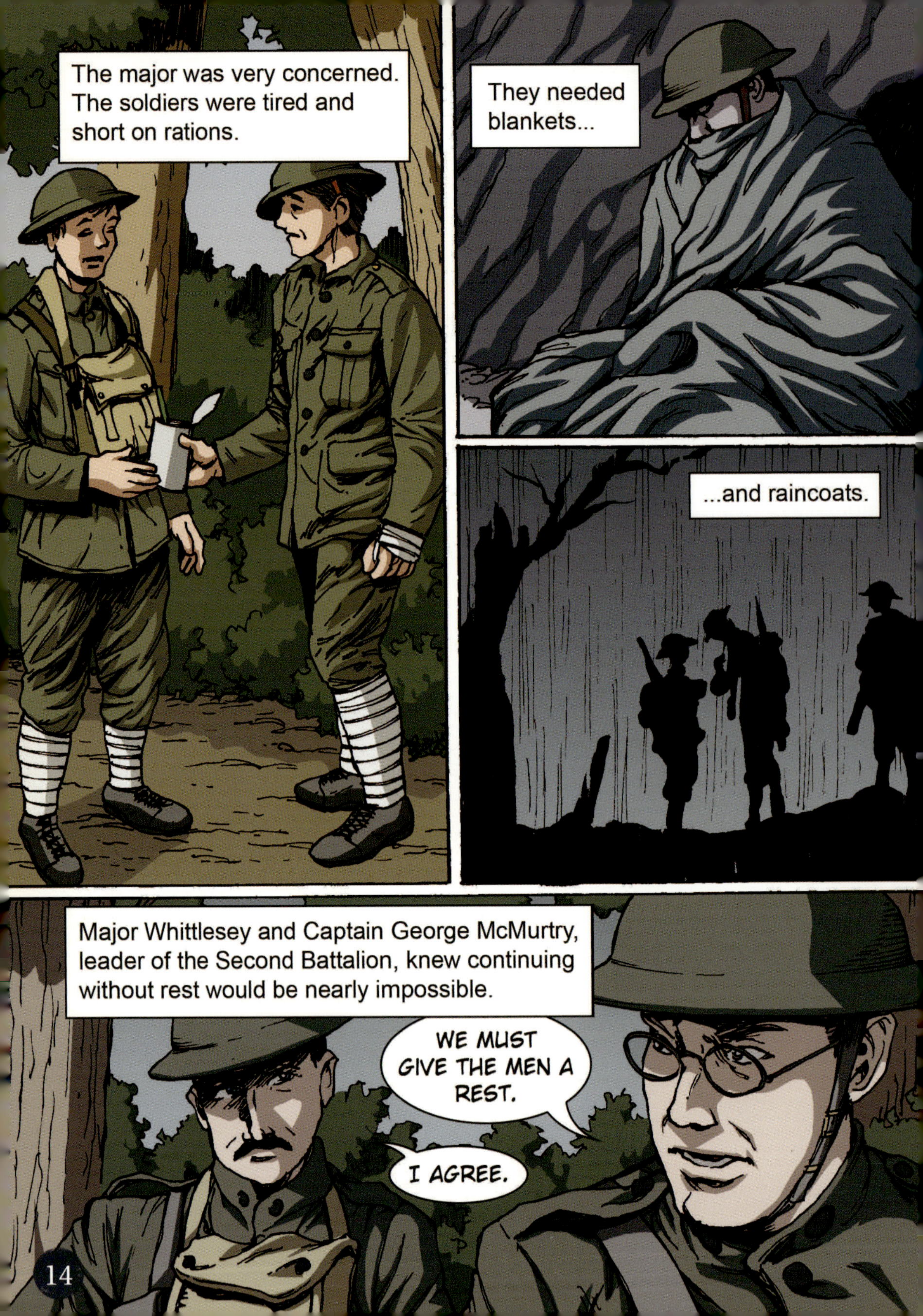
The major was very concerned. The soldiers were tired and short on rations.
They needed blankets...
...and raincoats.
Major Whittlesey and Captain George McMurtry, leader of the Second Battalion, knew continuing without rest would be nearly impossible.
WE MUST GIVE THE MEN A REST.
I AGREE.

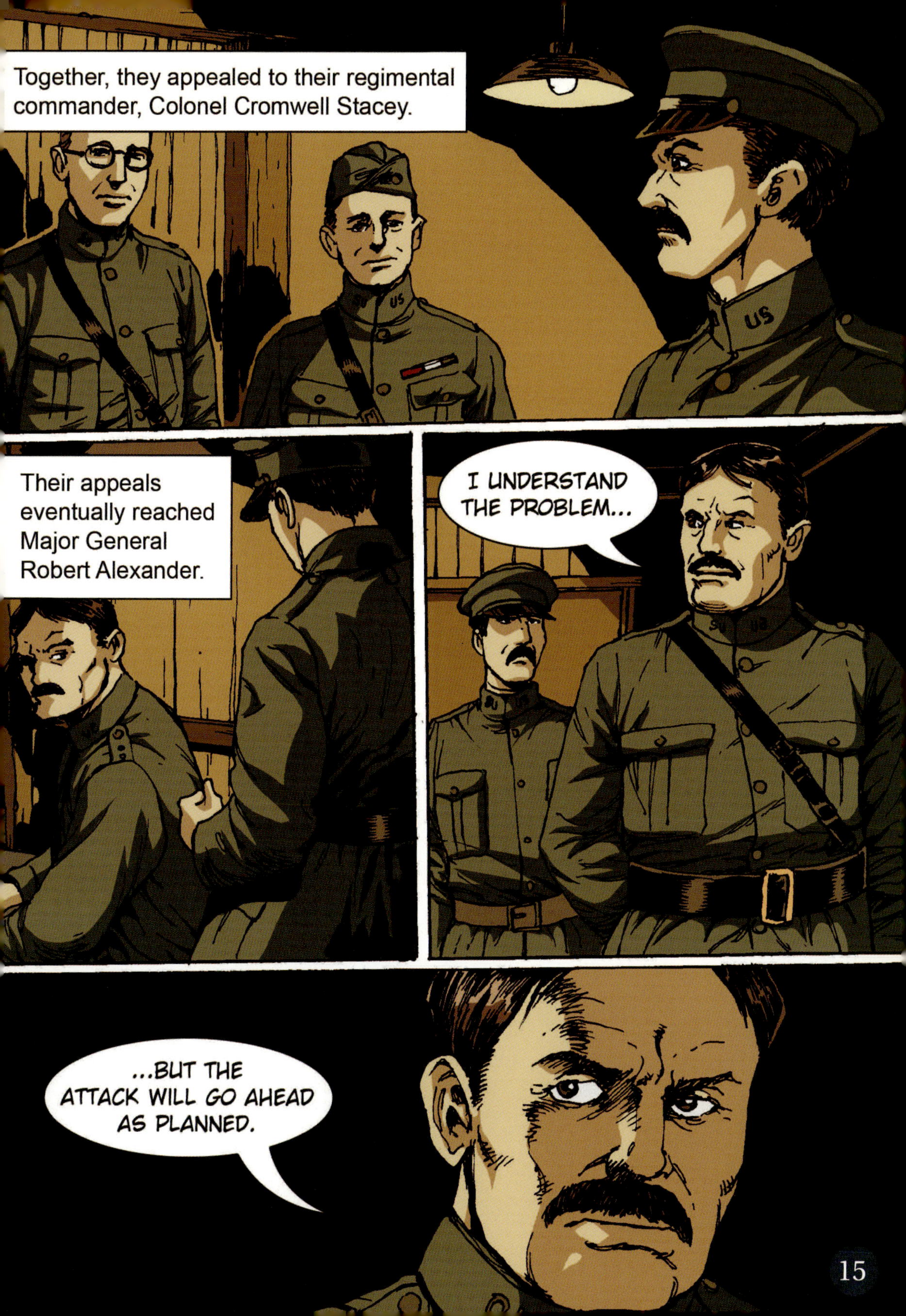
Together, they appealed to their regimental commander, Colonel Cromwell Stacey.
Their appeals eventually reached Major General Robert Alexander.
I UNDERSTAND THE PROBLEM...
...BUT THE ATTACK WILL GO AHEAD AS PLANNED.

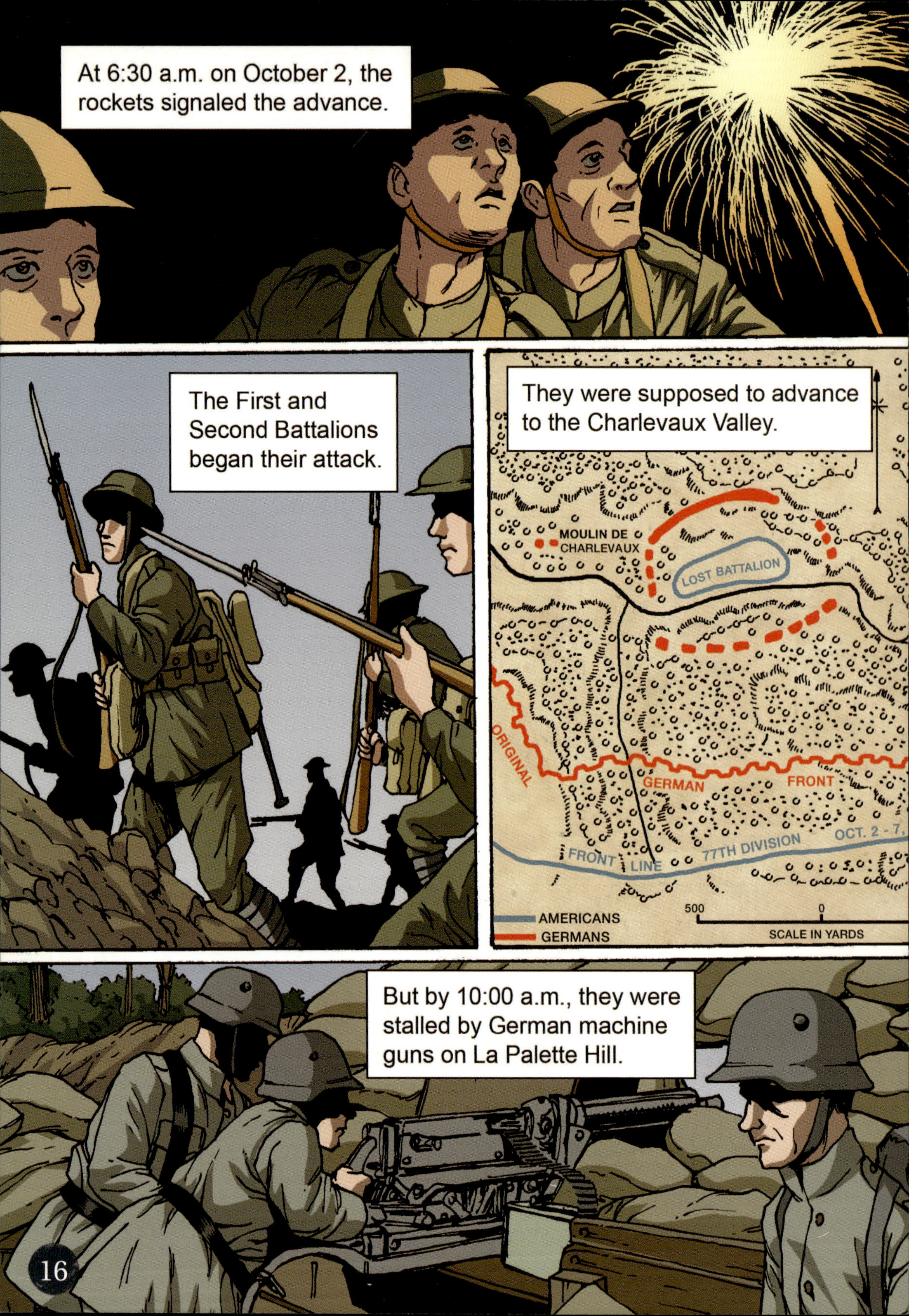
At 6:30 a.m. on October 2, the rockets signaled the advance.
The First and Second Battalions began their attack.
They were supposed to advance to the Charlevaux Valley.
MOULIN DE CHARLEVAUX
LOST BATTALION
ORIGINAL
GERMAN
FRONT
FRONT LINE
77TH DIVISION
OCT. 2 - 7,
AMERICANS
GERMANS
500
0
SCALE IN YARDS
But by 10:00 a.m., they were stalled by German machine guns on La Palette Hill.

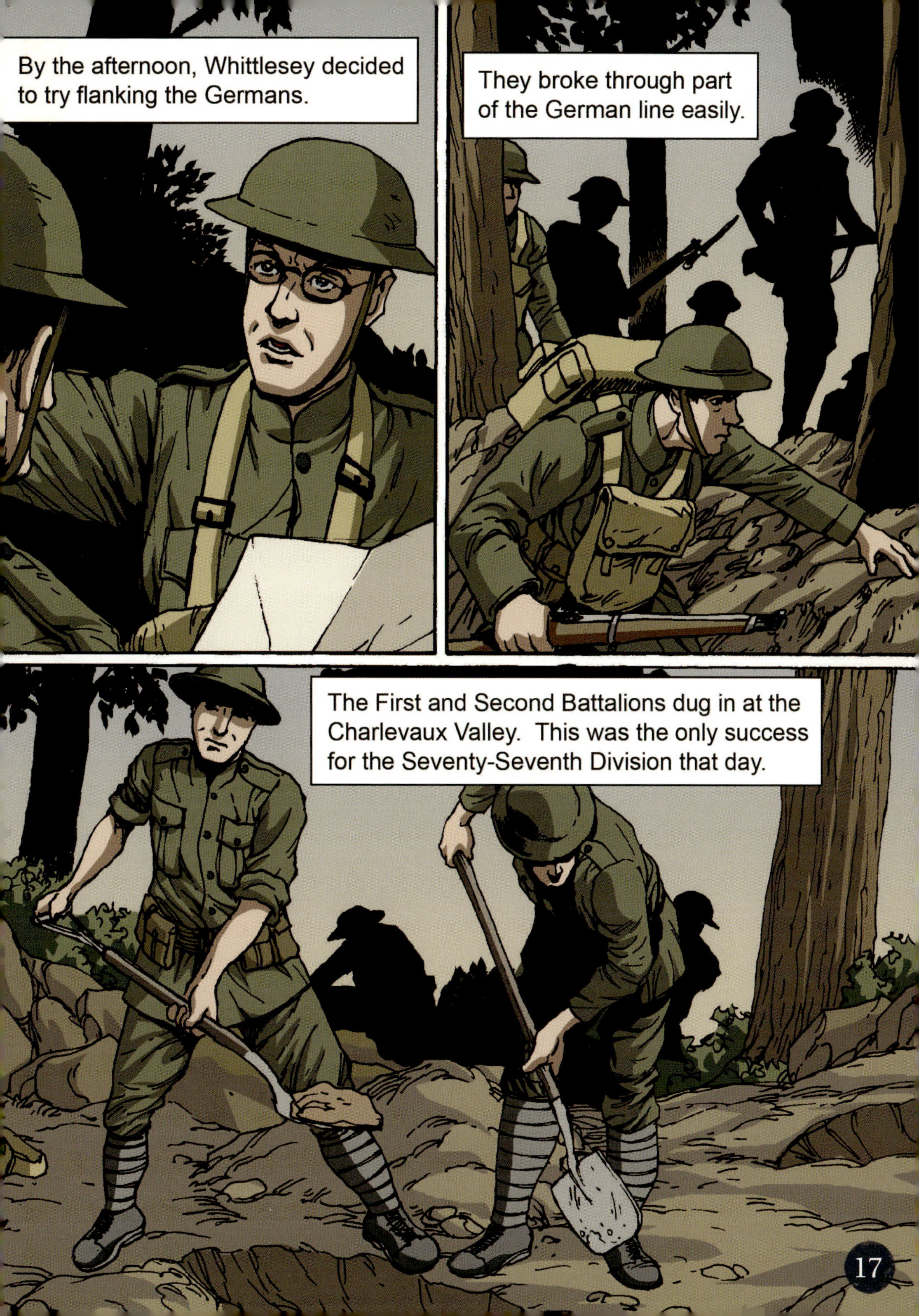
By the afternoon, Whittlesey decided to try flanking the Germans.
They broke through part of the German line easily.
The First and Second Battalions dug in at the Charlevaux Valley. This was the only success for the Seventy-Seventh Division that day.

CHER AMI TO THE RESCUE

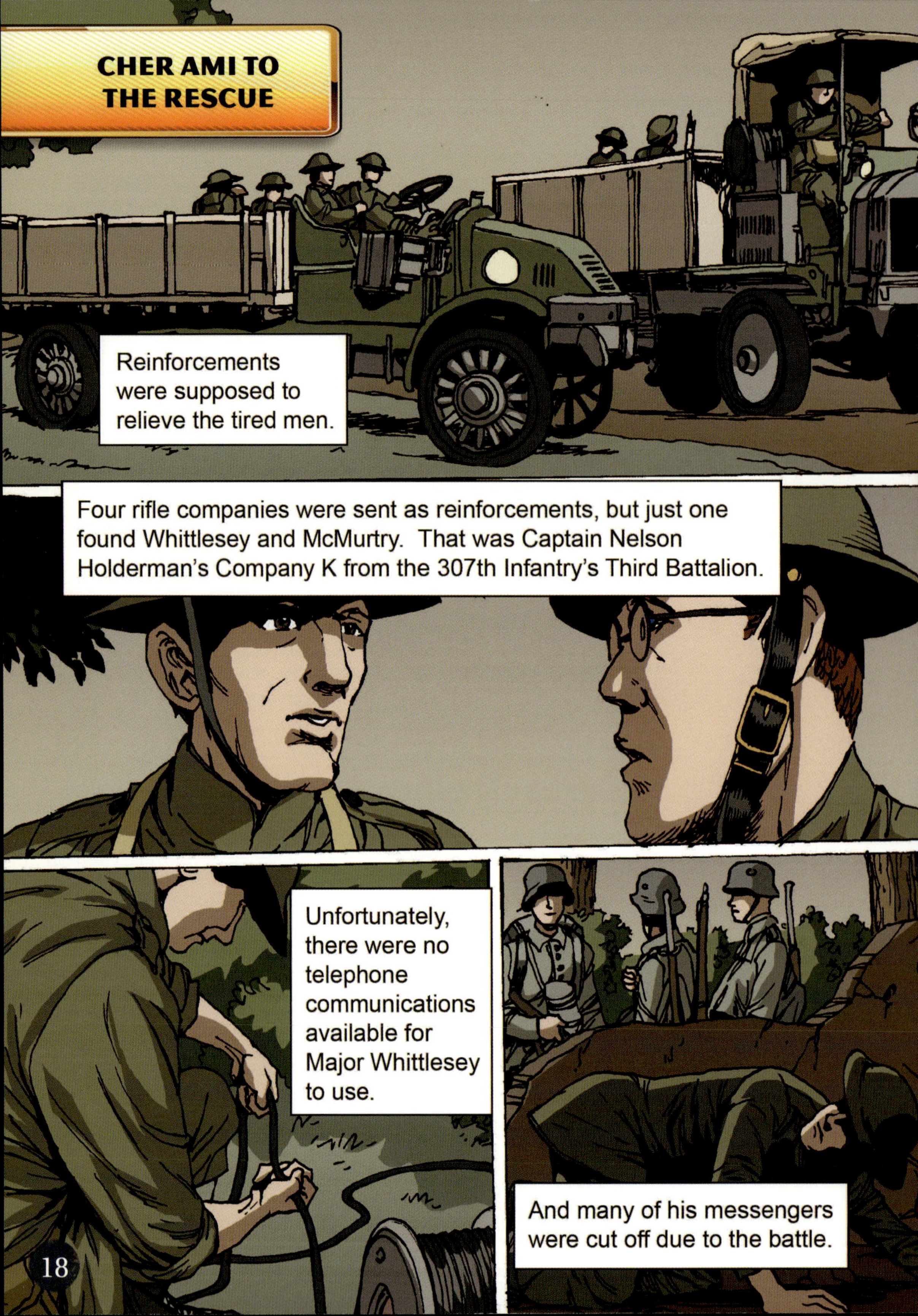
Reinforcements were supposed to relieve the tired men.
Four rifle companies were sent as reinforcements, but just one found Whittlesey and McMurtry. That was Captain Nelson Holderman's Company K from the 307th Infantry's Third Battalion.
Unfortunately, there were no telephone communications available for Major Whittlesey to use.
And many of his messengers were cut off due to the battle.

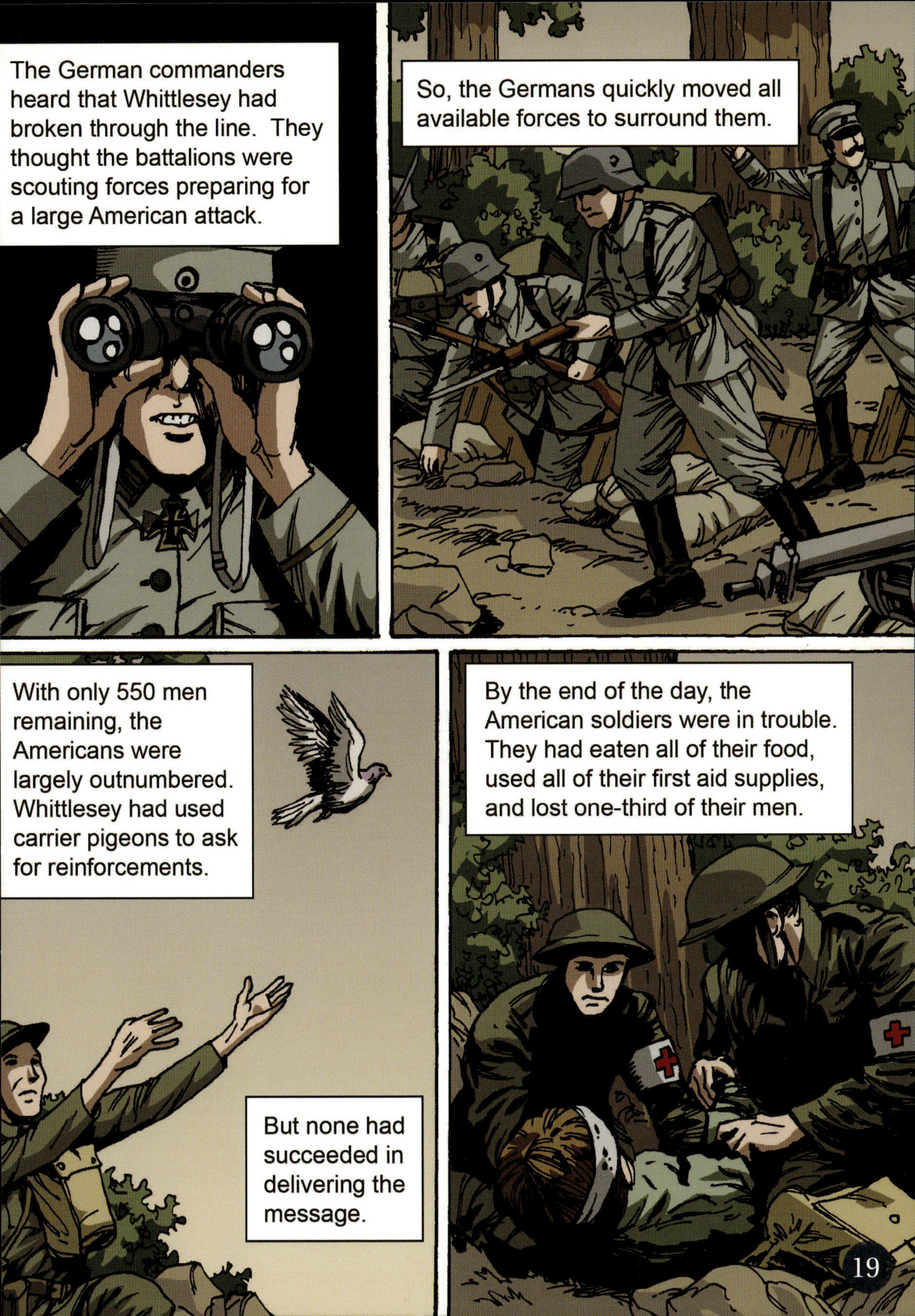
The German commanders heard that Whittlesey had broken through the line. They thought the battalions were scouting forces preparing for a large American attack.
So, the Germans quickly moved all available forces to surround them.
With only 550 men remaining, the Americans were largely outnumbered. Whittlesey had used carrier pigeons to ask for reinforcements.
But none had succeeded in delivering the message.
By the end of the day, the American soldiers were in trouble. They had eaten all of their food, used all of their first aid supplies, and lost one-third of their men.

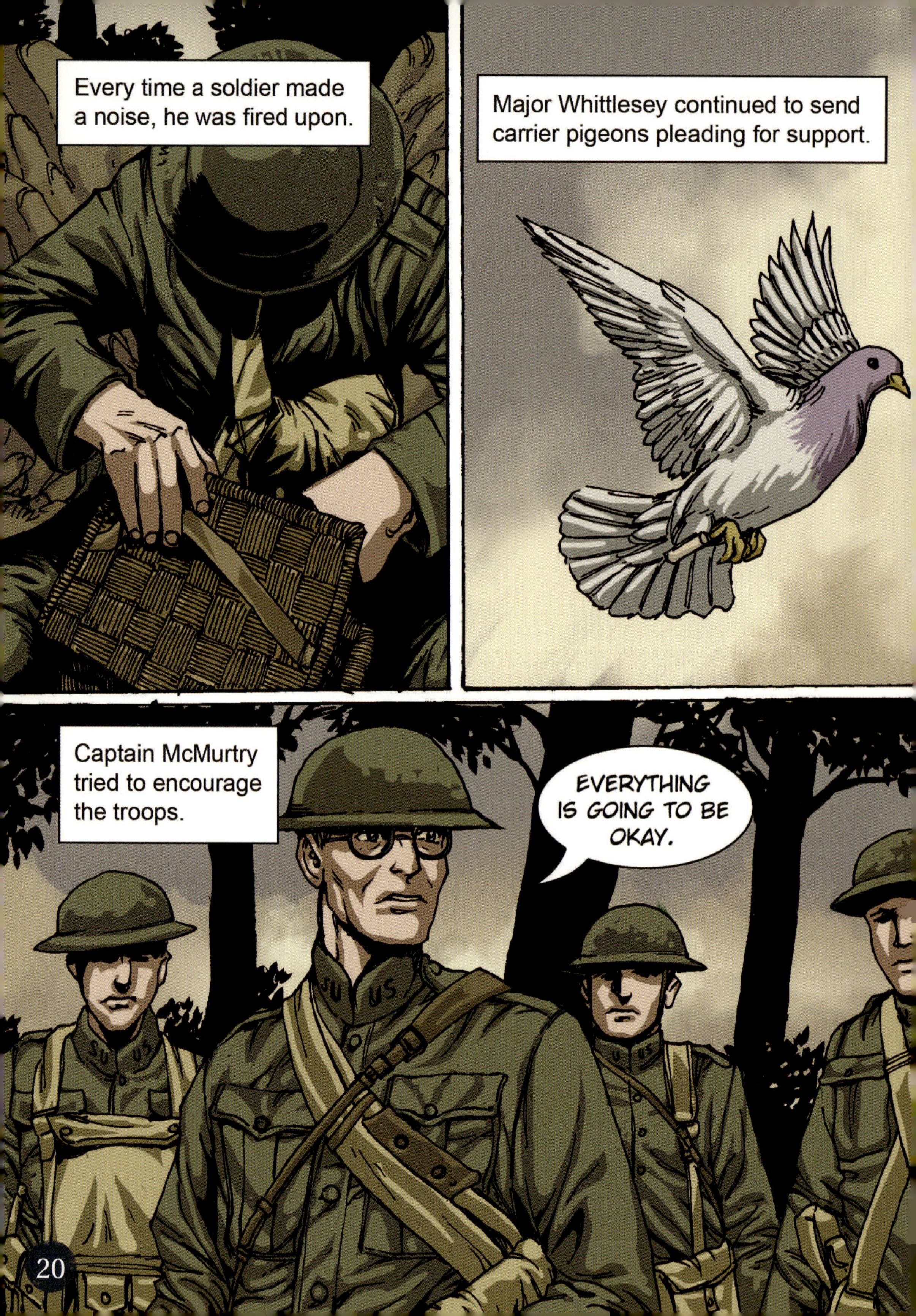
Every time a soldier made a noise, he was fired upon.
Major Whittlesey continued to send carrier pigeons pleading for support.
Captain McMurtry tried to encourage the troops.
EVERYTHING IS GOING TO BE OKAY.

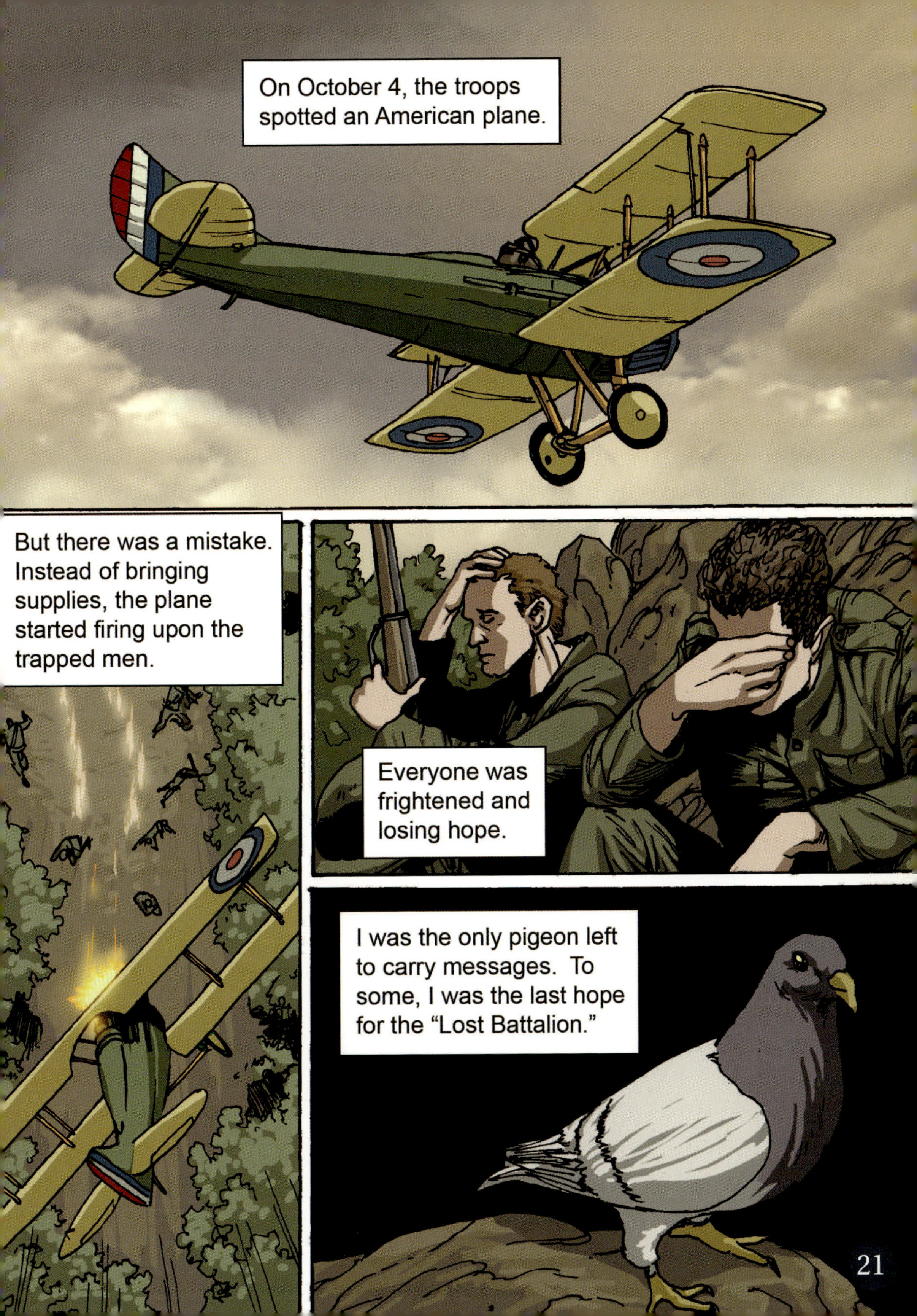
On October 4, the troops spotted an American plane.
But there was a mistake. Instead of bringing supplies, the plane started firing upon the trapped men.
Everyone was frightened and losing hope.
I was the only pigeon left to carry messages. To some, I was the last hope for the "Lost Battalion."

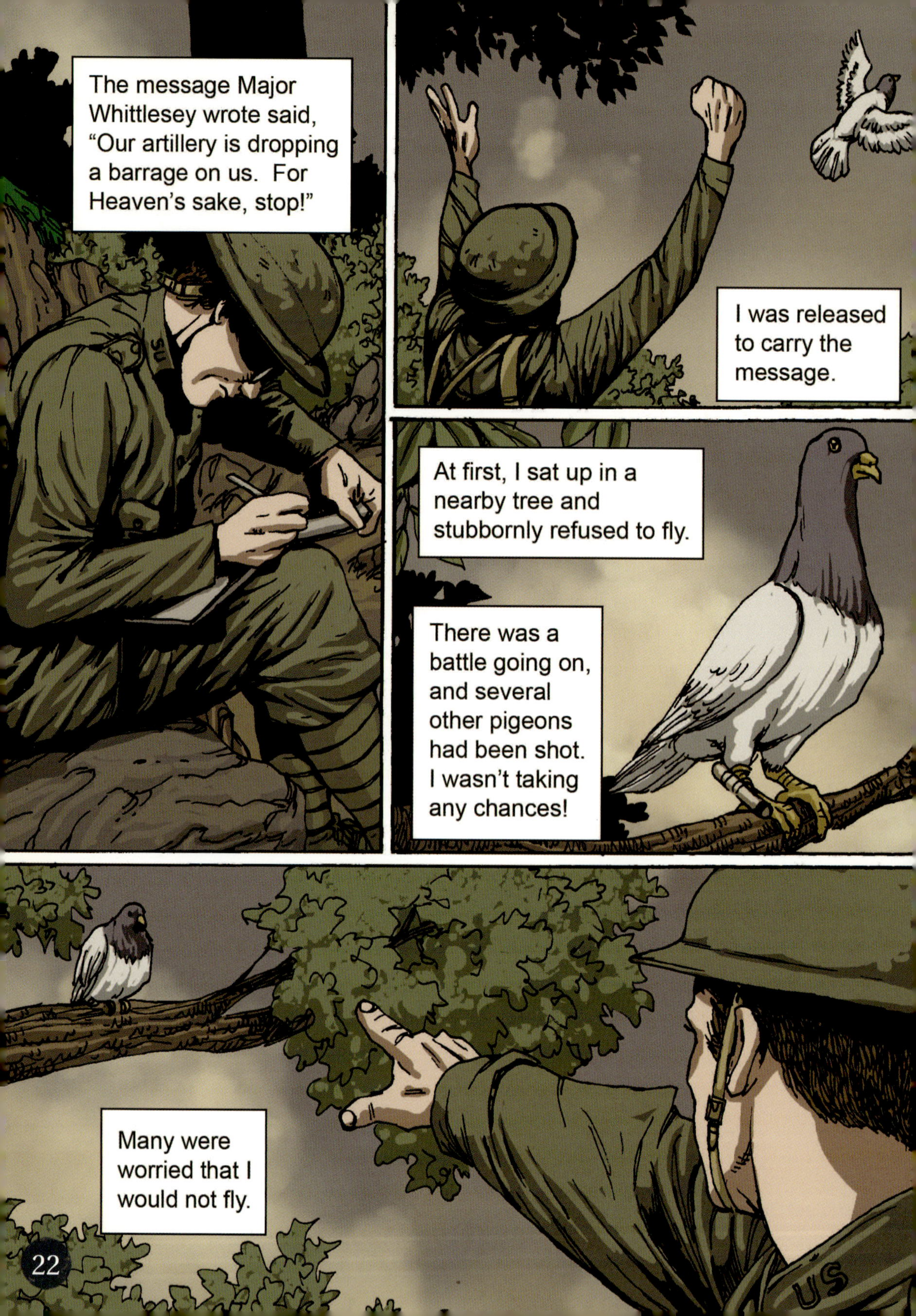
The message Major Whittlesey wrote said, "Our artillery is dropping a barrage on us. For Heaven's sake, stop!"
I was released to carry the message.
At first, I sat up in a nearby tree and stubbornly refused to fly.
There was a battle going on, and several other pigeons had been shot. I wasn't taking any chances!
Many were worried that I would not fly.
US

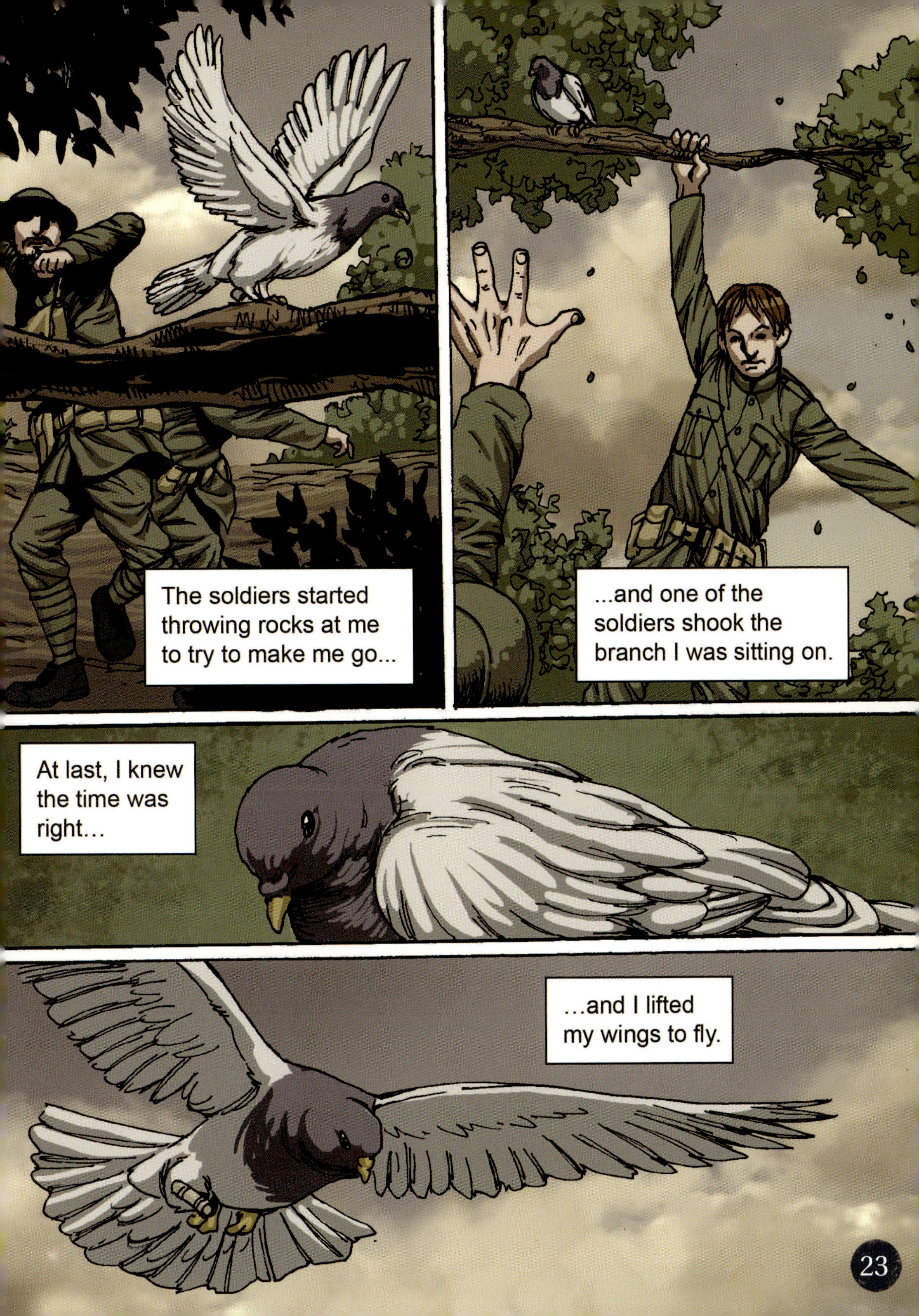
The soldiers started throwing rocks at me to try to make me go...
...and one of the soldiers shook the branch I was sitting on.
At last, I knew the time was right…
…and I lifted my wings to fly.

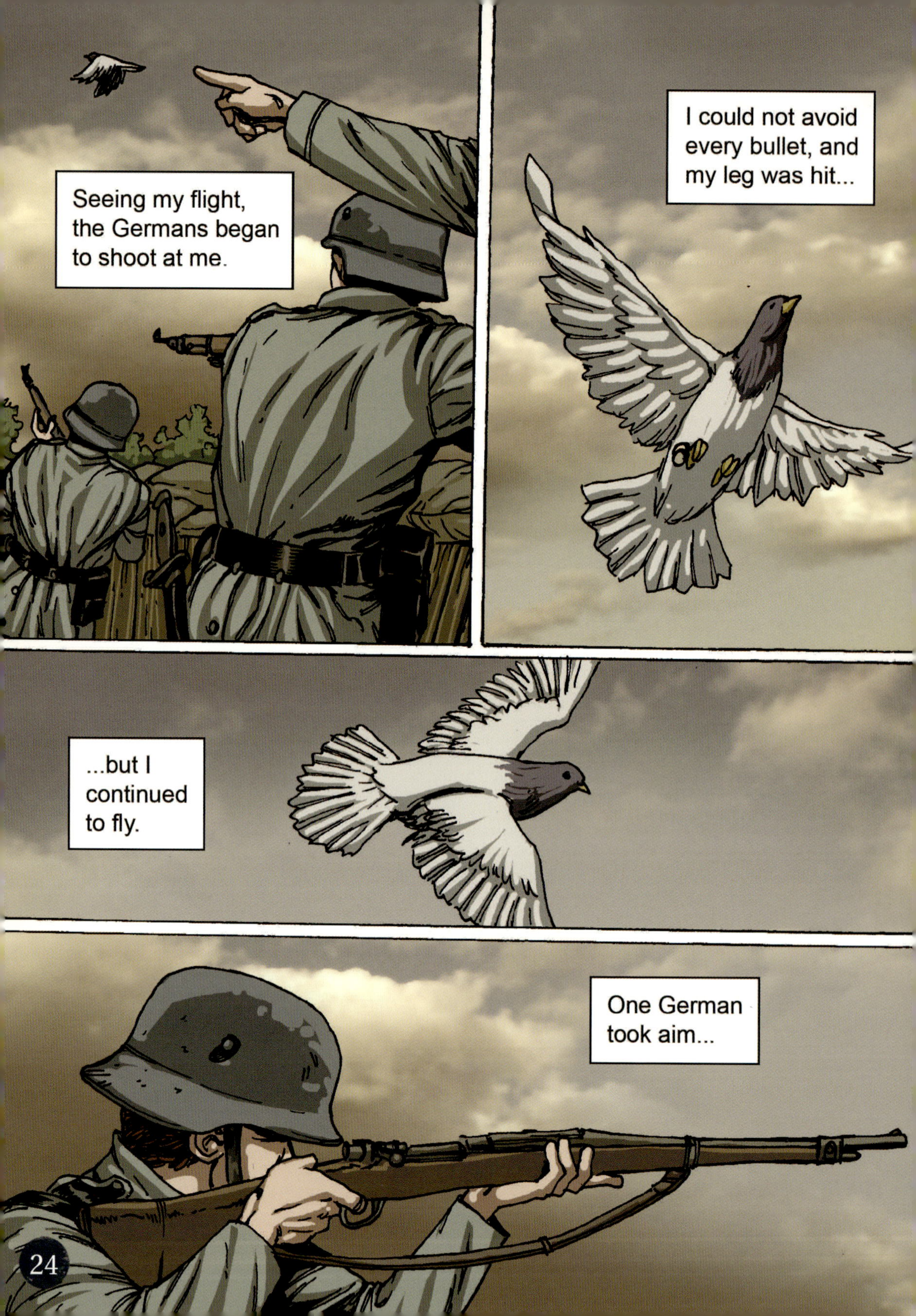
Seeing my flight, the Germans began to shoot at me.
I could not avoid every bullet, and my leg was hit...
...but I continued to fly.
One German took aim...

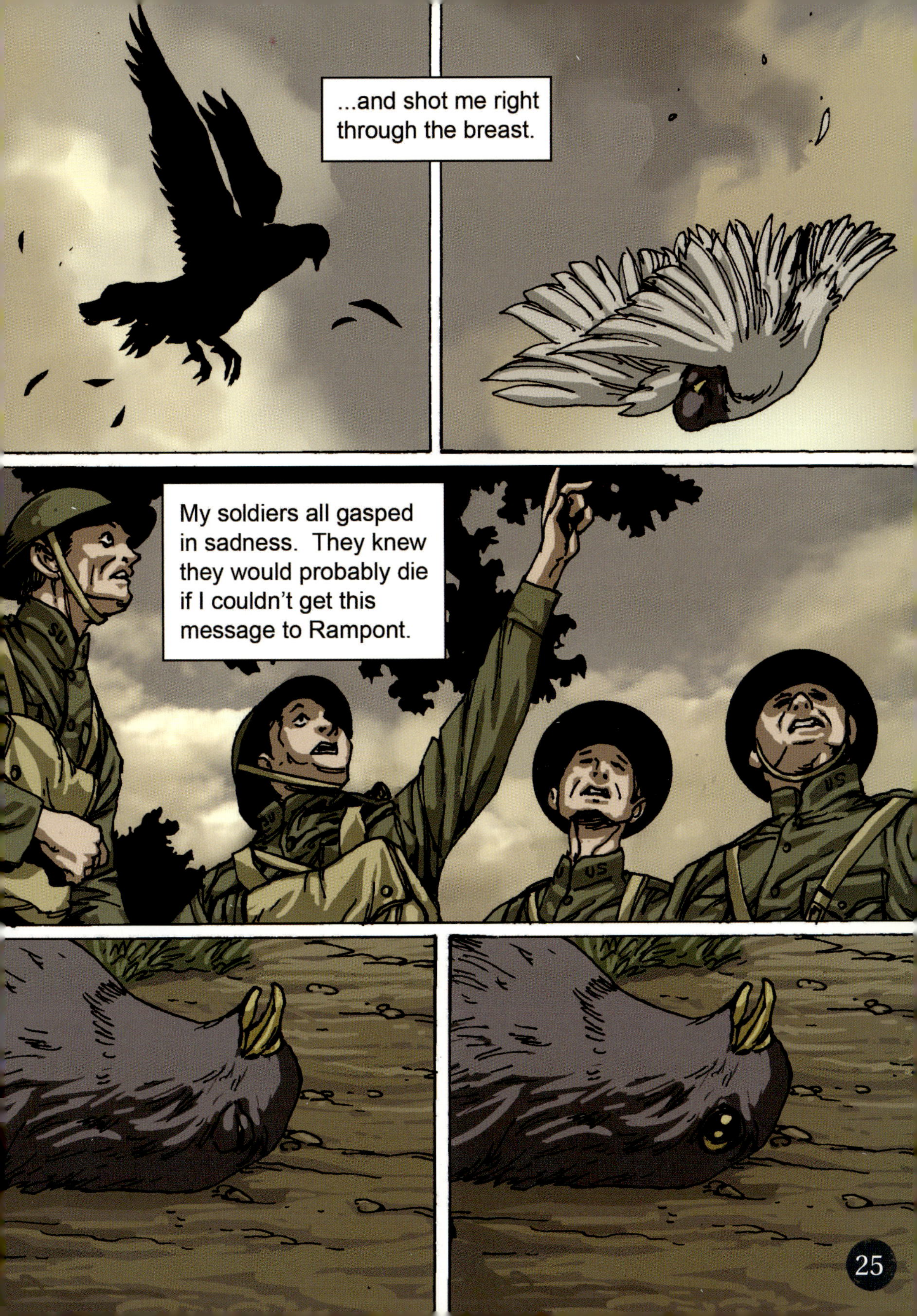
...and shot me right through the breast.
My soldiers all gasped in sadness. They knew they would probably die if I couldn't get this message to Rampont.

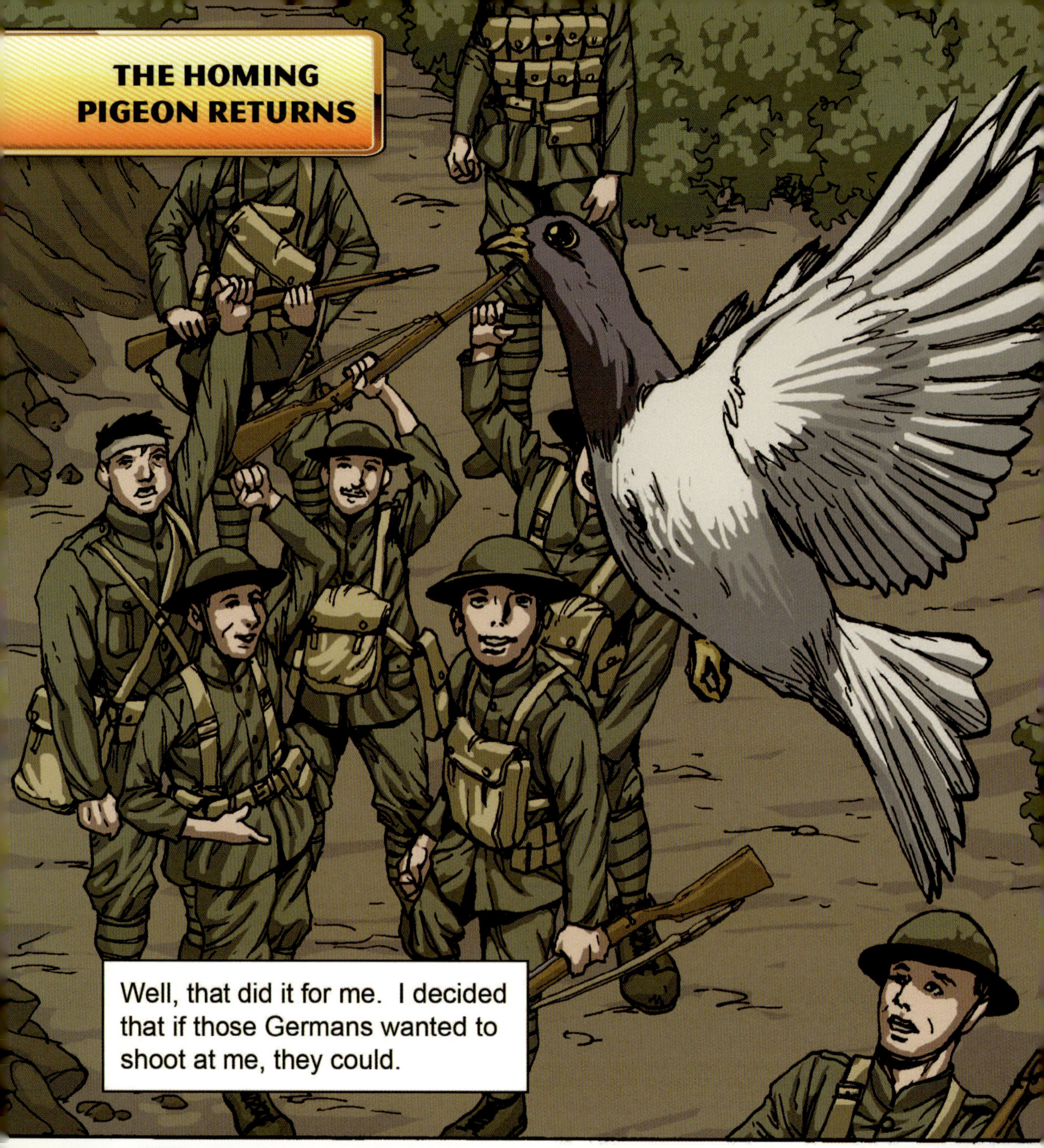
THE HOMING PIGEON RETURNS
Well, that did it for me. I decided that if those Germans wanted to shoot at me, they could.

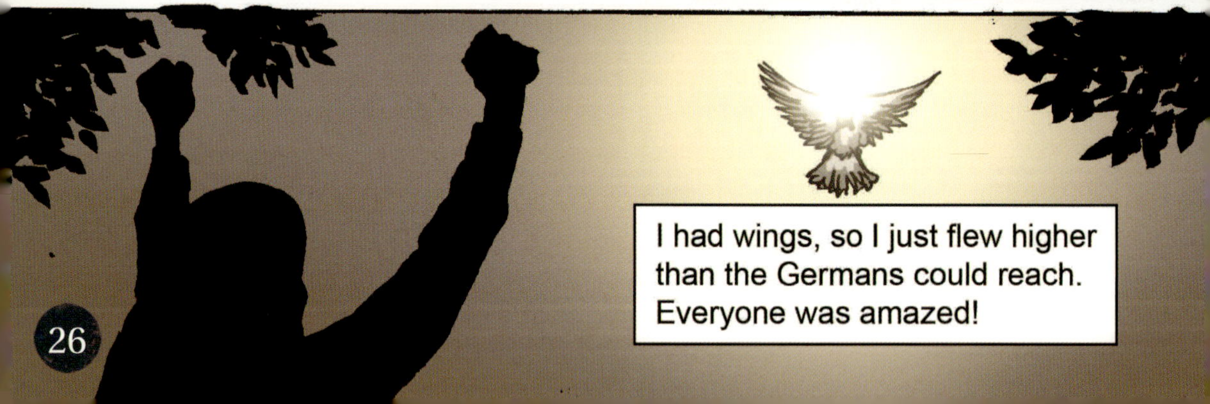
I had wings, so I just flew higher than the Germans could reach. Everyone was amazed!

I flew as fast as I could to Rampont, going 25 miles (40 km) in 25 minutes. That's almost an entire marathon in one-fifth the time of a normal runner.

I fell into my coop, ringing the bell that called a soldier to get my message.

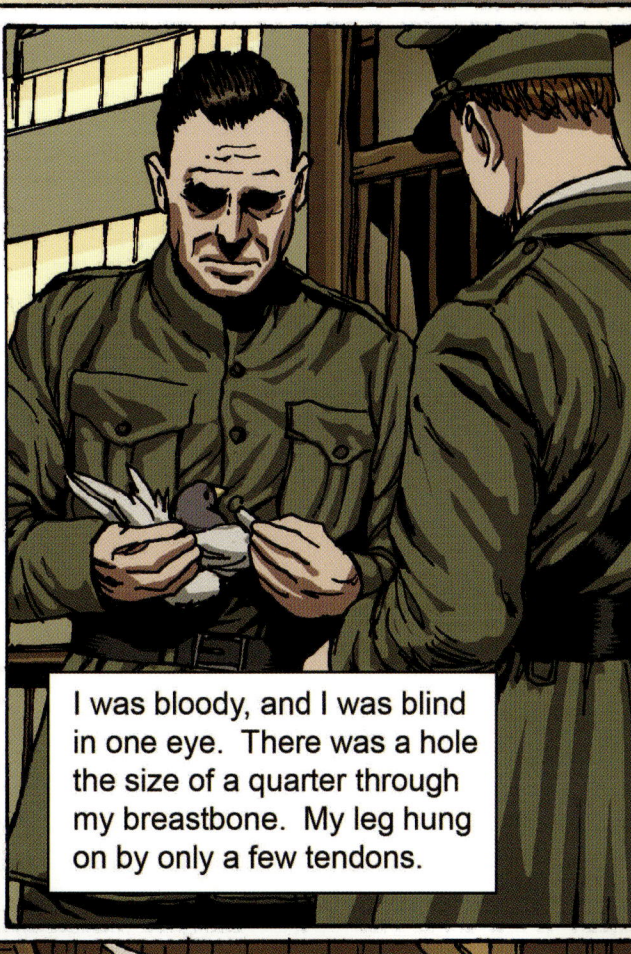

I was bloody, and I was blind in one eye. There was a hole the size of a quarter through my breastbone. My leg hung on by only a few tendons.

But the message had arrived.

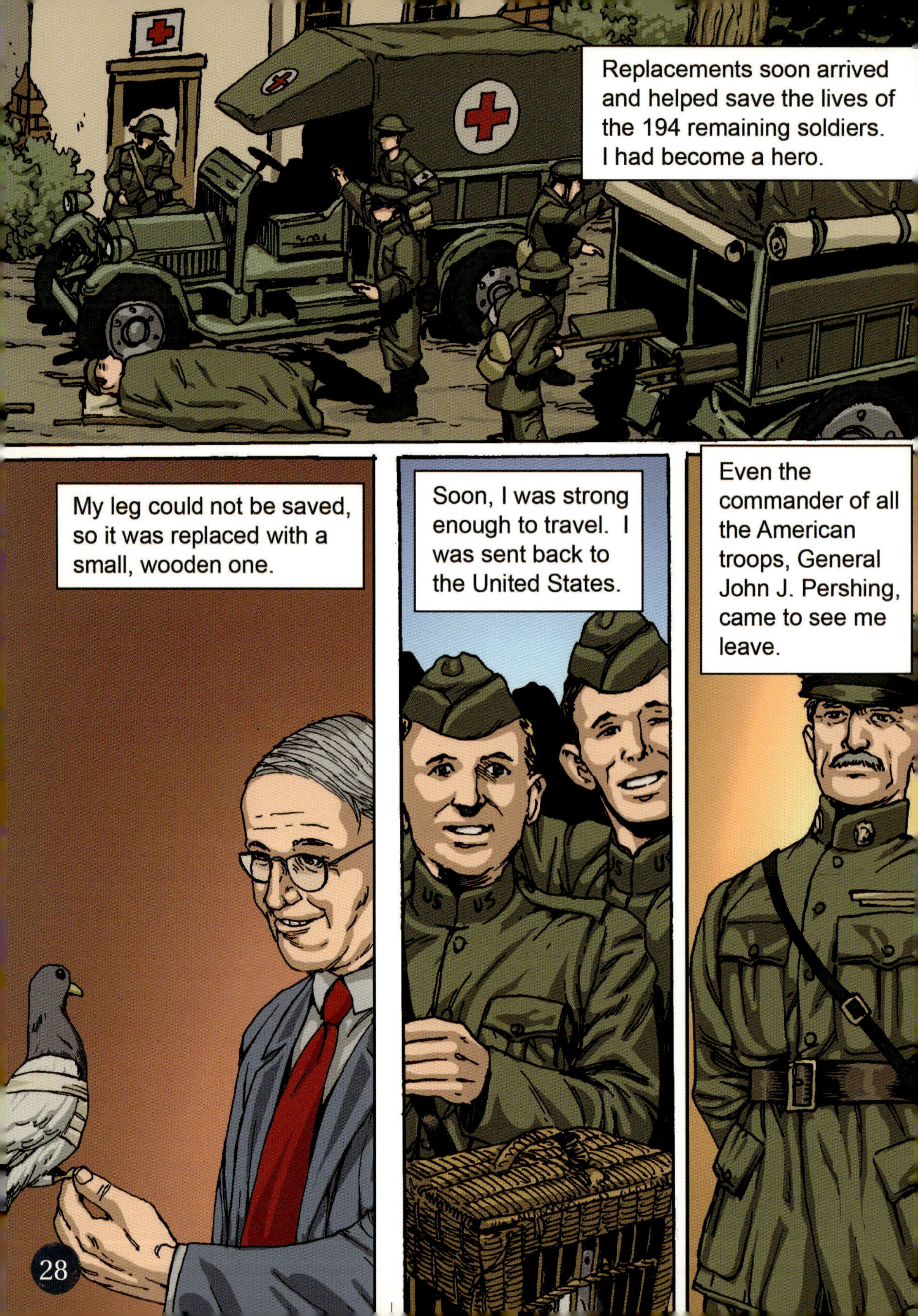
Replacements soon arrived and helped save the lives of the 194 remaining soldiers. I had become a hero.
My leg could not be saved, so it was replaced with a small, wooden one.
Soon, I was strong enough to travel. I was sent back to the United States.
Even the commander of all the American troops, General John J. Pershing, came to see me leave.
US
US

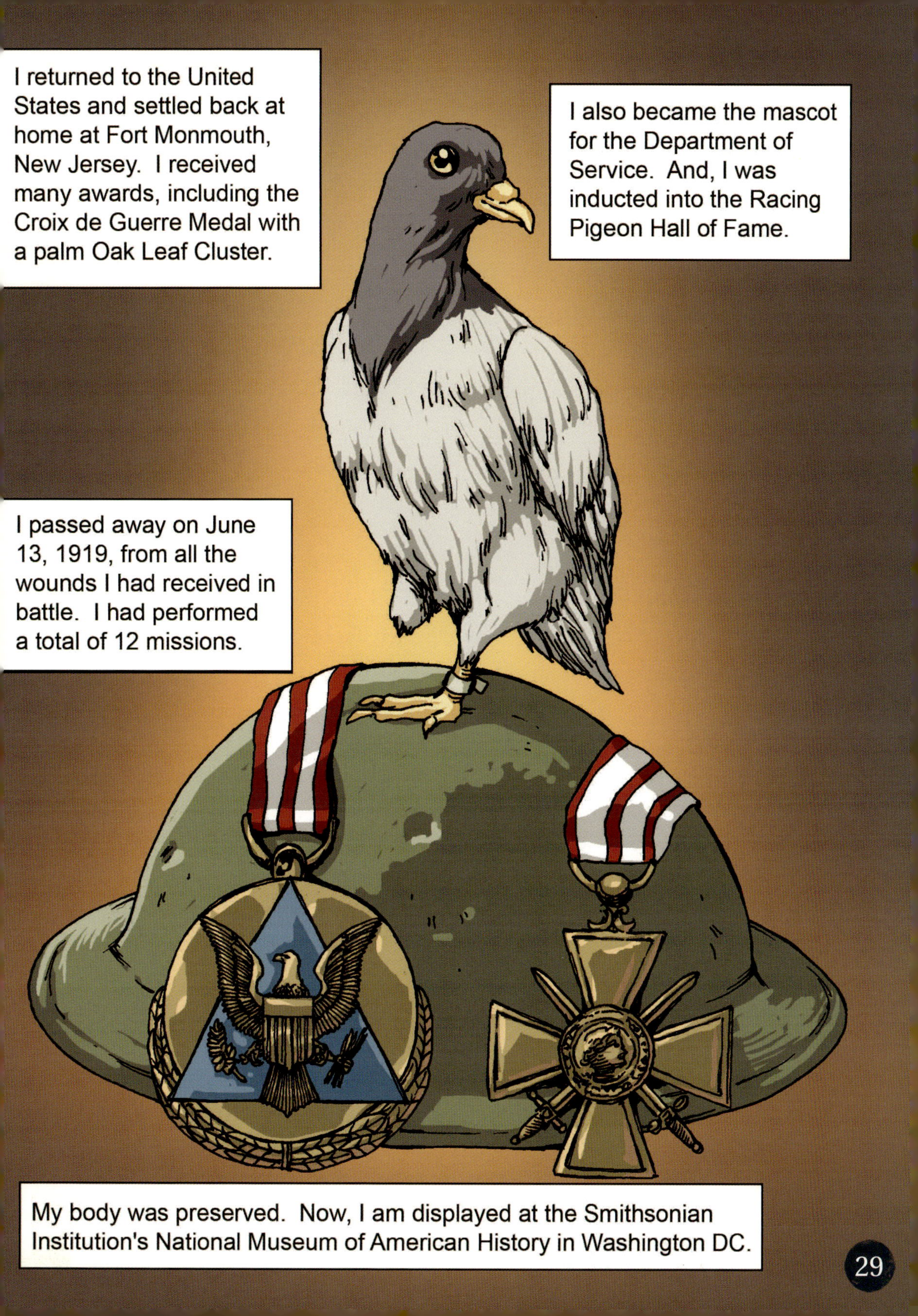
I returned to the United States and settled back at home at Fort Monmouth, New Jersey. I received many awards, including the Croix de Guerre Medal with a palm Oak Leaf Cluster.
I also became the mascot for the Department of Service. And, I was inducted into the Racing Pigeon Hall of Fame.
I passed away on June 13, 1919, from all the wounds I had received in battle. I had performed a total of 12 missions.
My body was preserved. Now, I am displayed at the Smithsonian Institution's National Museum of American History in Washington DC.

CHER AMI FACTS

Name: Cher Ami
Age at the time of the journey: Unknown
Weight: Unknown
Breed: Black Check cock carrier pigeon
Death: June 13, 1919, from wounds received in battle

Feats: Cher Ami delivered 12 important messages within the American sector of Verdun in World War I. The most well-known flight saved hundreds of soldiers in 1918.

Result: Cher Ami proved homing pigeons could be a useful message system and saved the lives of hundreds of soldiers.

WEB SITES

To learn more about Cher Ami, visit ABDO Group online at **www.abdopublishing.com**. Web sites about Cher Ami are featured on our Book Links page. These links are routinely monitored and updated to provide the most current information available.

GLOSSARY

artillery – a branch of the military armed with large firearms, such as cannons or rockets.
assassinate – to murder a very important person, usually for political reasons.
barrage – a line of weapon fire used to stop an enemy and protect one's own soldiers.
battalion – a large group of troops organized to act together.
coordinate – to bring into a common action or movement.
division – a military group that is part of a larger unit.
flank – to be on both sides of a group.
induct – to admit as a member.
mascot – something to bring good luck.
mobilize – to assemble and make ready for war.
preserve – to keep in its present state.
ration – a fixed amount of food.
regimental – relating to a military unit.
reinforcements – additional soldiers, ships, or supplies for military action.
relieve – to release from a post or job.
sabotage – harm caused by damaging or destroying something on purpose.
stalemate – a condition where neither side can win.
technology – using scientific knowledge for practical purposes, especially in industry.
tendon – a band of tough fibers that joins a muscle to another body part, such as a bone.
treaty – an agreement.

INDEX

A
Alexander, Robert 15
Argonne Forest 12
Austria-Hungary 5, 6
awards 29

C
Charlevaux Valley 16, 17

D
death 29

E
England 6

F
Ferdinand, Francis 5
France 6, 10, 12, 25, 27

G
Germany 6, 12, 16, 17, 19, 24, 26

H
Holderman, Nelson 18

L
La Palette Hill 16

M
McMurtry, George 14, 15, 18, 20

P
Pershing, John J. 28

R
Racing Pigeon Hall of Fame 29
Richards, Omer 13
Russia 5, 6

S
Serbia 5, 6
Smithsonian Institution 29
Stacey, Cromwell 15

T
Tollefson, Nils 13

U
United States 9, 11, 19, 21, 28, 29

W
Whittlesey, Charles W. 11, 13, 14, 15, 17, 18, 19, 20, 22